Beyond the Box

Innovative churches that work

Bill Easum
&
Dave Travis

Group

Loveland, Colorado

Group's R.E.A.L. Guarantee to you:

This Group resource incorporates our R.E.A.L. approach to ministry—one that encourages long-term retention and life transformation. It's ministry that's:

Relational
Because learner-to-learner interaction enhances learning and builds Christian friendships.

Experiential
Because what learners experience through discussion and action sticks with them up to 9 times longer than what they simply hear or read.

Applicable
Because the aim of Christian education is to equip learners to be both hearers and doers of God's Word.

Learner-based
Because learners understand and retain more when the learning process takes into consideration how they learn best.

Beyond the Box
Innovative Churches That Work
Copyright © 2003 Bill Easum and Dave Travis

Visit our Web site: **www.grouppublishing.com**

Credits
Creative Development Editor: Paul Woods
Chief Creative Officer: Joani Schultz
Editors: Gary Wilde and Candace McMahan
Copy Editor: Lyndsay E. Gerwing
Art Director: Kari K. Monson
Print Production Artist: Joyce Douglas
Cover Art Director/Designer: Jeff A. Storm
Cover Photographer: Daniel Treat
Production Manager: Peggy Naylor

Unless otherwise noted, Scripture taken from the HOLY BIBLE, NEW INTERNATIONAL VERSION®. Copyright © 1973, 1978, 1984 by International Bible Society. Used by permission of Zondervan Publishing House. All rights reserved.

Library of Congress Cataloging-in-Publication Data
Easum, William M., 1939-
Beyond the box : innovative churches that work / Bill Easum and Dave Travis.
    p. cm.
  Includes bibliographical references.
  ISBN 0-7644-2536-6 (pbk. : alk. paper)
  1. Church renewal. 2. Leadership--Religious aspects--Christianity.
  I. Travis, Dave, 1961- II. Title.
BV600.3.E27 2003
250--dc21   20030019
45

10 9 8 7 6 5 4 3 2 1   12 11 10 09 08 07 06 05 04 03

Printed in the United States of America.

Dedications

This book is dedicated to my daughter, who has taught me much about the emerging world.

—Bill Easum

This book is dedicated to Robert Springer, my maternal grandfather. Until his death in 2001, he served as a great role model of ministry in regular, faithful ways to those under his influence. To Evan A. "Bud" Abbott and Forrest C. Garrard, Jr., pastors in my formative years, who taught me that creative and caring ministries can work together to lead a church forward. Their untimely deaths left holes in my life that others have now filled.

To Elsie Fitzgerald, my paternal grandmother. At ninety-two years of age, she still faithfully serves the Lord in a variety of ministries in her church and her community. My grandparents and parents have taught me that everyone is gifted and everyone should serve. To W.T. Updike, who hired me to be his helper in denominational work thirteen years ago when I was a twenty-eight-year-old staff pastor. He taught me how to relate and work with a wide variety of church leaders. I continue to value his friendship and guidance. To Jim Martin, my pastor for almost twenty years. His long ministry in one place with one congregation shows the great fruit that can come from taking a long view. I am thankful to God that these leaders are still modeling and mentoring me and others in God's kingdom work.

—Dave Travis

Acknowledgments

Sharing the stories and principles of effective congregations isn't a solo effort. Both of us have many colleagues, friends, and supporters to thank.

I (Bill) am deeply indebted to the leaders of the churches included in the studies on which this book is based. May they continue to contribute to the growth of the kingdom.

I (Dave) would first like to thank the hundreds of church leaders we've met through our ministries in the past several years. These leaders, only a few of whom have been mentioned in this volume, give us great hope for the future of the church in America. Many have freely given of their time and influence to make this a better book.

Second, I must thank a few of my longtime present and former colleagues in the shared ministry of Leadership Network. Linda Stanley, Warren Schuh, and Cindi Haworth served on several teams relating to the specific churches mentioned in this book. My colleagues and friends Carol Childress, Greg Ligon, and Brad Smith have served with me on other teams, and I am indebted to them for their various contributions. In addition, Gayle Carpenter and Tom Wilson have provided much encouragement through their leadership. Bob Buford's generosity and encouragement make the whole organization work.

I must also thank my immediate family. Lynne, Stephanie, and Claire lost quite a bit of my time this year to the book project but encouraged me each step of the way. My parents, Ken and Jeane Travis, have always encouraged my intellectual, physical, and spiritual development by providing me with good models and untold opportunities. Mama always said I would be the storyteller in the family.

This is my first venture in book writing, and Bill Easum has done most of the heavy lifting, with constant rewrites and additions to my material. I am thankful he had the experience to keep the project on track.

Finally, we both thank the editorial team at Group Publishing. Gary Wilde served as our able editor and Candace McMahan as the supervising editor. Here's to more good work in the future.

—Bill Easum and
Dave Travis

Table of Contents

Foreword

The future belongs to churches that understand that healthy growth comes not through addition but through multiplication! You multiply your leaders by building teams and empowering every member for ministry. You multiply your impact by partnering with other churches. You multiply your evangelistic outreach by creating multiple services, multiple styles, and even multiple sites. You multiply the kingdom of God when you plant other churches.

For twenty-three years we've practiced these and other principles of multiplication at Saddleback Church. As a result we've witnessed God bless the church with exponential growth beyond our wildest dreams. Now there are many other churches that are modeling these principles, and this wonderful book is filled with examples.

I love this book because it is written by friends of mine about friends of mine. This is not theory. I can personally attest that these guys are actually doing what is explained in this book, and they are experiencing God's blessing. My prayer is that reading this will stir you to think and act "beyond the box," just as my friends have. Don't be afraid to go out on a limb—that's where the fruit is!

—Rick Warren
Author of *The Purpose-Driven Life* and *The Purpose-Driven Church*

Introduction
Thinking Beyond What Was

"You have heard that it was said...but I tell you..."
—Jesus of Nazareth

They gathered in a beautiful retreat center nestled in the rolling hills of North Carolina. A small group of Episcopal priests, wanting to explore the world of Gen-Xers, became engrossed in a dialogue. One of the priests said, "I guess if you want to reach Gen-Xers, you have to think outside the box."

Without hesitation, the Gen-Xer facilitating the discussion replied, "What box? We don't have a box. You have to think *beyond* the box."

At a time when many churches are just beginning to try to think *outside* the box, the rapidly emerging world calls Christian leaders to move *beyond* the box itself. Not to see around the box or go through the box or even get outside of the box, but to progress beyond it—to live and lead as if the box doesn't even exist.

What Is "Beyond the Box" Thinking?

Many people are writing these days about "out of the box" thinking or "coloring outside the lines." Neither of these issues is our main concern. We're writing about something much more radical. We are writing about people who believe, act, and live as if the box never existed.

As we tested the material in this book, we noticed that many people failed to catch the critical distinction between "out of the box" and "beyond the box." Most of us seem to be trying so hard to climb "out" of our own boxes that we simply can't grasp the idea of "beyond." We've also noticed that the minds of "in the box" and "out of the box" people are cluttered with so much box baggage that many of their questions don't have much meaning anymore. That is, they assume that certain things are normal or natural for Christianity—things such as hierarchy, structure, organization, property, location, conflict, centralized control, ordination, clergy, seminaries, and denominations, for example. Most of their questions flow from such assumptions.

The sad part is that most in- or out-of-the-box people are seldom aware that they are carrying this baggage around with them. In fact, a lot of thriving congregations aren't anywhere near beyond the box. They may be *out* of the box but not *beyond* it. Much of their world is still swirling with assumptions, causing them to waste their potential fighting battles that no longer matter.

So we're not talking about thriving leaders or churches. We're talking about leaders and churches that are oblivious to the box and are setting a brand-new course for the future. They are doing things that haven't been done in a long, long time. They are calling all of us back to a first-century Christianity.

To convey the radical nature of beyond-the-box faith, we've compiled a three-column chart depicting the shifts from "in" to "beyond" the box:

In the Box	Out of the Box	Beyond the Box
Stuck and dying	Thriving and growing	Radically innovative
Property is important	Relocate or expand	Property agnostic
Looking for help	Holistic growth	Pursuing opportunity
Interventionist/restart	How to grow our church	Missionary mind-set
Survives/protects heritage	Institutional effectiveness	Kingdom orientation
Struggles	Grows	Plants new ministry
Organization, polity, control	Decentralized	Reproductive
Maintains	Adds	Multiplies
No DNA	Unembedded DNA	Gives DNA away
Culturally ignorant	Invites public in	Goes out and sends
Protects heritage	Willing to be adaptive	Radical innovation
Controlling	Benevolent hierarchy	Gospel is everything
Elects slot fillers	Trains key leaders	Models leadership
Avoids change	Comfortable with change	Embraces change
Chaplain	Career	Missionary/apostle
Slave to constitution	Ignores constitution	Flexible guidelines
Members	Volunteers	Discipled servants
Staff are doers	Staff are equippers	Equipping culture

You can probably add a few columns of your own, but by now you catch our drift. So when questions emerge as you read, ask yourself, "From which column(s) do these questions arise?" Are they in-, out-, or beyond-the-box questions? Then do your best to avoid trying to answer those that come from "in" the box. And realize that even those "out" of the box are cluttered with a lot of box baggage.

> *We believe that the five essential mind-set changes addressed in this book will chart the course for Protestant Christianity for the next three decades.*

The truth is that none of the things in the first column have anything whatsoever to do with biblical Christianity. It's time for us to acknowledge this and move on to important issues that will advance the kingdom of God. In other words, it's time to think beyond one-person leadership that merely equips a team. And it's well past time to think beyond one church, beyond existing in a "sacred" location, and beyond the hope of merely planting another church.

We're offering a radical new vision. Are you beginning to see it?

Now you
see it.

Now you
don't.

Are You Thinking "Christendom" or "Christianity"?

In order to understand these concepts, you'll need an image of the church stripped of as much of the cultural "box" baggage of Christendom as possible.[1] With an understanding of the church shaped more by Christendom than by Scripture, you may find the contents of this book hard to swallow, perhaps even heretical. However, if you'll begin freeing yourself of the baggage of Christendom, you'll quickly see the biblical implications—and the possibilities— these concepts offer.

Most of Christendom associates leadership with seminary-trained professionals tethered to an institution called the church. Their primary responsibility is to manage the institution and take care of its membership. Maintaining the membership in the institution, more than accomplishing the mission given by Christ, defines their role. Members are entitled to privileges, one of which is to have primary access to the time and energies of the leaders. It's not unusual to hear churchgoers say, "This is *my* pastor." But this is a view from within the box.

Likewise, most of Christendom associates the word *church* with a place that must be managed by professional clergy. Churchgoers "go to church," invite people "to their church," and usually "love their church." Ask most churchgoers today, "Where is your church located?" and they will answer something like "At the corner of Main and Seventh." In many cases it's the property, more than the calling, mission, or opportunity, that dictates the form and amount of ministry a church can provide. For the same reason, in many new church starts, after a few months of moving around from place to place, sooner or later a well-meaning person will ask, "Pastor, when are we going to become a 'real church'?" He or she is really asking, "When are we going to build our own church building?" Again, this is a view from within the box.

However, leadership beyond the box is defined by mission, not place or professional status. Leaders are spiritual beings whose primary role is to equip and to ensure that those within their ministries have a safe environment in which to grow in Christ so that they can produce more Christians. Covenant replaces formal membership, and members become servants who are equipped to be ministers of Jesus Christ. This is the view from beyond the box.

In the first century, the word *church* related to the kingdom movement that went beyond time and space. Instead of a place, Christians loved their Christ. Ask a Christian in the first century, "Where is your church?" and his or her response would be something like "Wherever two or three of us gather together."

The early Christians invited their networks to gather with them and other Christians in their homes, catacombs, or wherever. First-century Christians didn't have a tethered view of the church; rather, calling and mission dictated the form and extent of ministry. This is the view from beyond the box.

From within the box, the word *church* refers to little more than an institution with a geographical location that must be managed by professional leaders. From beyond the box, Christians think of the church more as a movement untethered to a location. They also think of leadership defined by mission rather than place.[2]

Thus "moving beyond the box" means getting rid of the baggage of Christendom and rediscovering the original mission of Christianity—that is, fulfilling the Great Commission. The mission is not to establish local congregations as much as to spread the news of Jesus Christ across the world by every possible means.

In light of these contrasting approaches, let's chart some of the practical differences between the boxes of early Christianity and of Christendom. Consider:

Early Christianity & *Beyond* the Box	Christendom & *In* the Box
The church invisible	A visible local church
Birthed by the Holy Spirit	Chartered by a group
Is mission	Has a mission
Re-presents Christ to the world	Reflects denominational heritage
A communal and sent people	A place where something happens
Meets in many locations	Meets in one location
Informally gathers	Formally constituted
A city has one church, many locations	A city with many churches
Denominations aren't necessary	Denominations mean everything
A movement	Organized institutions
Redemption in Christ	Church membership
Role model the kingdom of God	Keep the institution viable
Servanthood	Entitlements
Leaders are missionaries	Leaders are professionals
Organism	Organization
Indigenous ministry	Ministry based on tradition

From these comparisons we can draw the following conclusions about the true mission of the church and its leadership. In the first century...

- telling the story of Jesus Christ to anyone who would listen was the essential characteristic of the early church—and should be today.

- the church was led by nonprofessional missionaries who traveled in teams. It's the kind of leadership needed today.

- Christians didn't set out to establish a form of organized religion. Nor should this be our purpose today.

- the church was more of a movement than an organized institution. It should be primarily a movement today.

- the church "happened" wherever two or three Christians gathered together. This is still the case today.

- the church didn't need any formal agreement of the people participating, formal membership, or a dispensation from a head office. It doesn't need such formalism today.

- the purpose of the church was to model and proclaim the coming of the kingdom of God. That is its purpose today.

A church does not have to be institutionally organized, though it can be. A church does not have to be part of a denomination, though it can be. In the early church, as long as whatever was done brought people to Jesus Christ, the form or style didn't matter, and it shouldn't today. In other words, this box called Christendom has had a profound impact on today's Christianity—and it shouldn't. It's time we moved beyond that box.

We've already mentioned that this movement will involve some crucial mind-set changes. What exactly are those changes? They make up the overall outline of this book, each chapter being dedicated to one of the five changes. We'll go in-depth about what each of them means in practical application. But for now, here they are in a nutshell:

Mind-Set Change 1: Shifting leadership from the one to the many.

Mind-Set Change 2: Moving from core-group to a culture of equipping.

Mind-Set Change 3: Thinking beyond one church to the "church in a city."

Mind-Set Change 4: Expanding the area of influence by going multisite.

Mind-Set Change 5: Progressing beyond *addition*-oriented church planting by developing *multiplication* movements.

How Do Beyond-the-Box Leaders Function?

Over the past decade, we've enjoyed being close observers and consultants with a host of leaders who are beyond the box. They're launching ministries that not only defy conventional wisdom but also seem to be "off the wall" to many of their colleagues. However, to those who are able to see beyond the box, their ministries just seem like a natural response to the Scriptures. Their efforts are opening up many new vistas of hope and possibility for ministry.

This new breed of leaders has one thing in common: *Mission is the mother of their theology.*[3] Everything they do is driven by one question: "If we do this, will it bring more people to faith in Jesus Christ and expand the kingdom?" They take seriously the admonition in 1 Corinthians 9:22 and are willing to try anything—even if it opposes social norms or goes against denominational traditions—to achieve this goal. More than having a mission, these churches *are* mission. Mission is their essence. These leaders understand that *not* to be missional is *not* to be the body of Christ.

After all, mission is not a mere function of the church; it is the natural expression of our life together in Christ. Every leader and every church are missionaries. To be the church is to be missionary. To have theology is to be involved in mission. These leaders are part of a divine movement throughout the world that is taking them (and, we hope, all of us) way beyond the local congregation. These leaders are teaching us much about the congregations of the emerging world.

We welcome you to an exploration of this exciting new movement. This book will invite you to know these Christian leaders and congregations who know nothing of the "box." Our hope is that you will be caught up in the movements God is spawning through them. Our sincere desire is to see churches just like yours stretch far beyond the box into true kingdom success.

"To the weak I became weak, to win the weak. I have become all things to all men so that by all possible means I might save some" (1 Corinthians 9:22).

—Bill Easum and Dave Travis
Winter, 2002–2003

How to Use This Book

This book contains two parts. Part 1 focuses on *leadership* issues, while Part 2 explores three major forms of *ministry* outreach to the world. The epilogue summarizes where we have been and what we have learned, and an appendix offers resources for further study and action.

We've inserted various "Timeout" sections in the chapters to help you apply the material to your unique situation. The questions there should help you create conversations among your leaders regarding key issues. We hope these will inspire you to develop practical adaptations unique to your church's needs and context. Pray as you read and discuss so that both your heart and mind will stay open to God's prodding. Also keep in mind that the term *directional leaders* refers to roles such as a senior pastor, who has directional responsibility for the church. The term *congregational leaders* refers to a multiplicity of leaders, both paid and unpaid staff, and those who provide special leadership to the whole body. We strongly urge you all to spend time together delving into the "Timeout" questions.

However, we don't expect every chapter to appeal to every reader. We suspect you'll be tempted to pick and choose the subjects that interest you. But we encourage you to read all of the chapters so that you might get caught up in the passion, commitment, and discipline of the leaders and congregations we highlight.

Nor do we want the book to be prescriptive in terms of detailed instructions. The leaders you meet in this book clearly have a sense of God's call on their lives and through the ministries they serve. That should be common with all God's servants. If God is not calling you to these specific ideas, follow God's particular call to you rather than our ideas.

However, we also believe that God is calling some of you who are fearful and tentative. This is understandable. Yet you still desire in your heart to see these types of movements in your place of ministry. Being exposed to these movements will help open your eyes to what God is doing around the country with others who have been similarly fearful. Their experiences won't necessarily tell you *how* to accomplish beyond-the-box changes, because no single way exists that is best for every situation. That's why the churches we mention in the book are real—and why our ideas flow from our observations and conversations with the leaders of these congregations. Unlike some books that dream up idealized versions of a church and hope for the best, this one is all about real life in real churches in North America.

When you finish this book, you can also go to a special Web site dedicated to this book's readers: www.easumbandy.com/beyondthebox. Try it out if you want to partner or enter into conversation with Bill or Dave about the issues that are so dear to all of our hearts.[4]

> *You can't fly with eagles if you spend all of your time being modeled by turkeys!*

About the Authors

Bill Easum, a former pastor in the United Methodist church, led a turn-around church in San Antonio for twenty-four years. When he left that ministry to enter the apostolic ministry of helping other leaders, the church was a large, thriving congregation. For the past fifteen years, Bill has led his own consulting group, working with all types of churches. He is still connected with his mainline tradition but desires to help his friends there see the possibilities that other churches are modeling.

Dave Travis was a staff pastor, a senior pastor, and a denominational executive for the Southern Baptists before joining the staff of Leadership Network in 1995. Leadership Network's calling is to identify, connect, and provide resources to innovative church leaders in the United States and Canada. In his current role as senior vice president, he oversees the ministry teams that serve churches. He comes from, and is still connected to, the evangelical wing of the Christian movement in America. But he also desires his tradition and friends to see the hopeful future that the innovative churches described in this book are shaping.

Endnotes

1. *Christendom* refers to the previous 1,600 years. For more on Christendom, see Bill Easum's *Leadership on the OtherSide: No Rules, Just Clues* (Nashville: Abingdon Press, 2000).

2. For more on the meaning of Christianity as a movement, see Bill Easum's *Unfreezing Moves: Following Jesus Into the Mission Field* (Nashville: Abingdon Press, 2002).

3. Martin Kahler coined the phrase some eighty years ago.

4. Our examples that follow are based upon information gathered in 2002 from personal and e-mail interviews, as well as written materials produced by the churches themselves. The churches and leaders we discuss in this book represent the best of many other churches or organizations. In a few negative examples, we did spare some embarrassment by not giving the names of those churches.

   If you'd like more conversation on the issues, go to www.easumbandy.com/beyondthebox.

Part 1
Leadership Beyond the Box

Are you a beyond-the-box leader? This section will help you find out. The leaders and congregations you'll meet in this section have adopted a Mental Map that is fundamentally different from that of inside-the-box and outside-the-box leaders.

In Chapter 1, you'll see what this means when it comes to your team-building efforts. The key challenge is this: *Can you give away personal ministry to a team of people?*

Chapter 2 takes you to the next step: equipping all of your members to move beyond the box in exercising their God-given gifts for ministry. Beyond giving ministry away to a team, a leader must ask, "How can I build a system of equipping throughout our entire congregation?"

> *Every person must see himself or herself as an equipper of other servants. This Mental Map begins with the key leadership and infiltrates the whole body of believers.*

Chapter 1
Beyond One-Person Leadership:

Shifting to Teams

"Hello, Dave? This is Ronnie Smith calling from Easter Church. I'm a deacon here, and Joan Rodgers, a friend of yours in our denomination, suggested you could help us with a problem."

"I'll try," I answered.

"Well, our church has seen tremendous growth over the past few years, and we're outgrowing our worship space. We have two services that are full, and now we're wondering whether we should rent an empty Wal-Mart building down the road where we can seat everyone in one service or maybe two. We can get it for a good price. What do you think?"

I first asked him about adding additional services at their present campus. But Mr. Smith talked about some issues they'd had in the past with attracting people to other worship times. Nevertheless, I began to see that the church really had plenty of capacity at its present site. I had no objection at all to their using the empty Wal-Mart building for worship or even fully relocating there. But I didn't see this as the real issue.

"Why don't you have worship at *both* sites?" I asked.

"Why would we want to do that?"

"Why not?"

"Well, I guess because two of our leaders wouldn't go for it."

I paused before offering a wild guess: "Is it the senior pastor and the worship pastor?"

Mr. Smith hesitated for a minute and then admitted it.

"So what you're telling me," I said, "is that the key capacity constraint is not really space. It's the unwillingness of the senior pastor and worship pastor to lead worship at additional times or to recruit another team to do so."

"Yeah, I guess that's it."

"Well, you're normal. But you'd better get beyond that way of thinking."

I talked with Ronnie for a few more minutes, sympathizing with this perplexed staff member. The whole system was built around what the two pastors thought they could personally handle. Their limit was two services, on Sunday, at a specified time. They were unwilling to consider having additional services or not being the primary leaders of those services. My guess is that their other leaders would have seen the issue in a similar way. They would have said, "We can't do that because we don't want to burn out our pastor."

But suppose the church's leadership supply wasn't limited by *individual* constraints? Suppose the church moved to *team* leadership?

Will You Take Up the Team-Building Challenge?

Ronnie Smith's church is like many other inside-the-box congregations in North America. It continues to build bigger buildings in order to meet the desires of one or two staff members and a few other key constituents, even though it probably costs much more to do so over the long haul. At Easter Church, all they had to do was begin thinking beyond single person–centered leadership to a different way of leading. In doing so, they would not only solve their space problems, but also avoid many of the long-term church health problems that typically afflict a growing congregation's life and ministry.

The problem is that they had fallen for a crippling delusion—the myth of the heroic leader. You've probably heard the refrain: Everything rises and falls on leadership. For most churches, this means that everything rises and falls on the senior pastor. Although it's true that the senior pastor is a key element in the equation that leads to strong churches and kingdom impact, the myth is that *everything* depends on him or her. Many senior pastors themselves have succumbed to the heroic leader myth and placed themselves into dysfunctional expressions of leadership because of it.

Church boards have also bought into the myth. They do this when they place too much responsibility for the church's overall health at the feet of the senior pastor. He or she gets too little credit when things go right and all of the blame when things go wrong. Then, functioning like boards of directors for businesses or professional sports teams, these church boards "fire the coach" rather than build a coherent team strategy.

Part of the problem relates to the nature of church organization itself. Church leadership is usually highly visible in public gatherings, where all eyes are on the people "up front." Because preaching and worship-leading are public roles that produce powerful images, many in the congregation equate those images with leadership. But does this equation add up?

In his book *Good to Great*, Jim Collins writes about fifteen companies that advanced from being good to great. The leaders of these companies are not household names, are not well covered in the media, and have not written "tell all" books to publicize their accomplishments. He also names several CEOs with whom everyone in America is familiar. These folks are seen as strong, innovative leaders who have driven their organizations to the forefront of national attention. But even though these leaders' names are instantly recognizable, their companies' performance levels lagged behind the fifteen comparison enterprises.

Collins and his researchers found a qualitative difference in the types of leaders within the compared companies. The top-performing companies followed "Level 5 leaders," whom Collins defines as persons who "channel their ego needs away from themselves and into the larger goal of building a great company. It's not that Level 5 leaders have no ego or self-interest. Indeed, they are incredibly ambitious—*but their ambition is first and foremost for the institution, not themselves.*"[1] These Level 5 leaders intentionally build up other leaders around them so that the leadership does not all fall to one person.

Other approaches may make it easier for observers to pick out an organization's leader. And it makes a good story to hear of the heroic, lone church-planting couple who enter an area and build a great church. Yet, as we have investigated such stories in depth, we've seen that the lone-ranger aspect has usually been exaggerated in hindsight. In virtually every case, God was going ahead to prepare not only a planter but also *a team of people who would carry out the vision.* Therefore, we believe that a critical mind-set change must occur: Senior pastors must lay aside their egos and the idea of being heroic leaders.

> **Senior pastors must lay aside their egos and the idea of being heroic leaders.**

We're not disputing the fact that the need for strong pastoral leadership is gaining wide acceptance today. It's not unusual for us to see senior pastors effectively exercising their gifts as directing leaders for a congregation. And we've seen tremendous growth in institutions and ministries that focus on growing the personal leadership gifts of church leaders. These ministries stress individual spiritual disciplines, control systems of time- and life-management, and overall personal development as central tasks. There is nothing wrong with these emphases. We all need development in these areas, and we are big fans of many of these ministries.

However, beyond-the-box churches are going further. They know that strong, centralized leadership is not enough. These churches develop teams of leaders that become part of the fabric of the church and give direction in many dimensions of their congregations. As you will see throughout this book, one of the key characteristics of these churches is the ability to envision and implement *multiplication processes* instead of focusing on simple addition. In this case, we are talking about multiplying a leader's gifts into a team of gifted people.

In other words, most pastors need to develop a culture of plural rather than singular leadership. Whereas in the past we had strong churches led by a primary single leader, now we see beyond-the-box churches with capable teams sharing the primary leadership. In-the-box leaders center leadership on themselves. Beyond-the-box leaders center leadership on the team. However, many senior pastors are reluctant to take themselves out of the limelight, and many church boards do not understand the importance of team ministry.

We have to get beyond the skill and ability of a few and tap the power of the many. In fact, one of the key differences between inside-the-box leaders and beyond-the-box leaders is this willingness and ability to build ministry teams. These churches give the majority control and direction to the teams and not just to a small group of leaders. The main obstacle is usually the senior pastor and his or her attitude toward letting go of control in order to empower and equip others.

During the last few years, we've noticed a growing movement toward multiple senior pastors and leadership teams leading some highly visible congregations. Those congregations may be identified with a primary communicator or lead pastor, but when we look more closely, we find a capable leadership team in charge. In most of these cases, an established team is giving primary leadership to the church. In such congregations, therefore, the phrase *follow the leadership* doesn't refer just to the senior pastor's leadership. It also points to the joint leadership of the pastors, staffs, lay pastors, and boards that are putting into action the God-given vision and mission of the church. The mission, vision, and direction flow from the top team into all of the church's ministries.

Let's look a little closer at this movement in order to see what exactly it takes to implement a team approach. We'll begin by surveying three kinds of essential empowerment.

Timeout!

For directional leaders (such as lead pastors):

• How much of your church's ministry is designed around you? What could you do to center more of it on others?

• How much ministry centers on a small group of individuals with visibility?

• Describe your church's "team at the top," and name its members. How many are "in leadership" based on their visibility rather than their leadership gifting?

For congregational leaders (such as paid and unpaid staff members):

• Describe the various groups that lead your church. Are they a team? Do they lead together? If not, why?

• What can you do to help these groups develop into a team? (Or do you need to find different people to lead these groups?)

• In what ways could you be limiting what God can do in your congregation by restricting the visible leadership to what a few leaders can accomplish? What could be done to overcome those limitations?

Can You Attempt the "Big Three Empowerments"?

Most out-of-the-box churches place one individual in the key roles of vision-casting, worship-leading, preaching/teaching, and providing pastoral care. Beyond-the-box churches decentralize and build teams for all of these functions. In order to do this, they build teamship at multiple levels in a variety of ways. Before we get into specifics about this, let's pause to reflect on two truths you'll need to keep in mind as you move into a more team-oriented ministry.

First, teams are biblical. Keep this truth constantly in mind. The New Testament abounds with examples of team ministries. At Antioch we find Barnabas, Simeon, Lucius, Manaen and Saul/Paul (Acts 13). Paul mentions his team members, either at the beginning or at the end of his epistles. There were times Paul's teams changed as he mentored and released individuals to return to places he had already been. Paul was a team-builder as he sought to build up the kingdom.

Second, working with teams is difficult. Especially in the areas of directional and public leadership, a team approach can be much more difficult at first. Be prepared for this. It's always easier for one person to make a decision and have the rest follow without question. In the long run, however, we have found that teams are much stronger than lone leaders. Leaders who build teams at multiple levels build more health and ministry capacity into their churches in order to accomplish the vision and mission. Teams can survive the ups and downs and crises much better than a few individual leaders can.

Now, what kinds of empowerment are required? For a church to move into authentic team ministry, the senior pastor and the governing body must empower three primary groups of people—the staff, the board, and the lay pastors. In our experience, the senior pastor must lead the process, and the board must give its consent, blessing, and encouragement.

Empowerment 1:
Enlarge and empower your paid and unpaid staff.

Previous generations of the old church-growth theory emphasized "staffing for growth." The theory was that staffing levels should always stay ahead of membership growth. That is, employing new, specialized staff persons would lead to growth in attendance. We can cite many cases in which this was the wrong strategy. In some cases, the individual employed wasn't interested in growing a ministry. In other cases, the individual came from another congregation that had a different culture, and he or she just didn't fit into the new environment. In still other cases, the wrong specialized ministry was attempted. For example, we've seen many churches employ staff persons for a singles ministry when the local demographics didn't warrant such a ministry. Even worse, most denominational systems require certain credentials for pastors if they're to serve a church. Many of these individuals train to be generalists, however, and do not have the tools to expand a particular form of ministry.

Beyond-the-box churches take another approach, consisting of these three aspects...

• **First, the majority of staff comes from within.** The character, spiritual growth, leadership capacity, diligence, and commitment to the church of these individuals have been observed over a period of time. They typically begin as unpaid staff within the church. At some point it's decided that they should be paid. Even then, it usually begins as a part-time position with the possibility of growing into full time.

Think about it. Can a search committee really select a good fit from just a few hours of interviews? Leaders coming from within the congregation already share the vision and heart of the church. They understand and support the direction of the church, and they've shown that they're headed in the same direction as the leadership. In addition, they've already demonstrated that they can handle leadership and its associated responsibilities. From the church's perspective, a task or role needs an identifiable leader, usually to develop and lead a team. Therefore a person isn't invited onto the staff in the abstract. A specific starting point or team exists; the person joins to do the things that need to be done. This task or role has a clear ministry description and a clear coaching and supervision structure.

Furthermore, the person understands the church culture and knows how things get done within that particular congregation. He or she already has a web of relationships, not only within the church but also within the community at large. Even in those instances in which someone joins the team from outside the congregation, the church makes sure his or her DNA truly "fits." In some cases, the senior pastor, the candidate, and the relevant team go on a retreat together to talk about the future of that ministry area. The person receives an offer to join *if* the team feels he or she is a good fit.

• **Second, other church leaders choose the staff members.** Many times this falls to the ministry leader closest to the new staff person. Sometimes it falls to the senior pastor. Those leaders not only select the new person but also train and equip him or her for ministry. Later they help evaluate performance to ensure that ministry is progressing. When there's need for correction and reproach, they are there as well. In some cases, the entire team hires and evaluates.

In-the-box leaders usually want to know how these people are trained theologically. The answer is, in various ways. Most of the beyond-the-box churches have in-house theological training courses. Many have partnerships with colleges and schools of ministry to deliver nearby or virtual training as well. Most important, they have on-the-job mentoring and modeling. (See the next chapter for more on this model.) We would put these "homegrown" leaders up against those educated in any seminary. We've found that leaders with extensive in-house training are usually more effective and theologically sound than those trained in more formal settings.

• **Third, the concept of "staff position" is significantly expanded.** In-the-box churches usually have a salaried model in mind. In a typical small church, the paid personnel may be the pastor, the worship leader, and the church secretary. A midsize church might add some worship staff, a youth director, a maintenance person, or an associate pastor to its list of paid staff. Larger churches might add another pastor and administrative personnel. If you were to examine an organizational chart, you would see a layer of staff, associate staff, volunteers, and then..."the people." This illustrates the number of layers between paid pastors and unpaid individuals. In other words, in-the-box churches continue to add layer upon layer of hierarchy to their systems.

As a practical example of how the beyond-the-box differences play out in real life, consider New Hope Christian Fellowship in Oahu, Hawaii (see www.enewhope.org). The leadership meetings there are for "everyone on staff," so the room is usually filled to capacity—with around a hundred people. Fewer than half of these folks receive a paycheck from the church. Yet each of them has a supervisor, a clear task, and access to the support functions such as office services, staff-training programs, and team-building activities. During the fifty-minute meetings, there is a time of worship, praise, prayer, vision-casting from some of the leaders, reminders of upcoming emphases, affirmations for jobs well done, and direction-giving for the coming weeks. In addition to these general staff meetings, there are team meetings for those in specific ministry roles. Whereas the general staff meeting is more presentational and devoted to vision-casting, the team meetings are more discussion- and task-oriented.

We have observed similar staff meetings in other churches. We've seen new church plants begin with five staff persons before the churches are launched. In most of those cases none of the staff, including the organizing leader, is paid by the church. The roles tend to include directional leader, administrator, worship leader, small-groups leader, children's leader, and youth leader. Each of these individuals may carry the title of pastor. Many of these roles grow into full-time paid positions over time.

If you are trying to make a transition to this approach, consider which persons in your church provide leadership to significant areas of the ministry, have a clear role, and have an accountability structure. Do these folks need to be added to your staff?

Timeout!

For directional leaders:

- List in writing exactly who is on "staff." Write a dollar figure or time factor next to each name.

- How many leaders are unpaid staff? Which teams do they lead? Or are they just "doers"? What teams *should* they lead?

- How can you begin equipping these folks to lead teams?

For congregational leaders:

- Using the descriptions above, how many "staff" people does your church really have? Who is paid? unpaid? Write down their names.

- What teams do these folks lead? Do all of your paid and unpaid staff carry within them the DNA of the congregation?

- Are the team players coached long enough that they feel secure in what they are doing? Do they feel as if they could contact you at any time for help? Do you coach them in how to recruit others? (Discuss the evidence that supports your responses.)

We've said that the first of the Big Three Empowerments is to enlarge and empower your paid and unpaid staff. However, you may be wondering what this will mean for you in the most practical terms. We'd like to suggest two initial steps you could take. The first involves simply observing and studying other ministries; the second moves you into looking at the benefits of expanding through internships.

- **Study examples of staff already functioning as teams.** At Leadership Network (see www.leadnet.org), we regularly survey senior pastors and other staff members involved with larger churches. One thing we've learned is that the average number of weekends in a given year that a senior pastor preaches or teaches is thirty-eight of the fifty-two weeks. In some of the largest churches, the number is much lower. The number is also lower for younger pastors and higher for those over sixty years of age.

This shift from the one preacher to many is one of the significant shifts of our time. It is the logical result of a world that requires team-based ministry. It clearly signals an end to the myth of the heroic leader.

Make no mistake, the senior pastors of these churches are generally the best communicators on staff. But they know several things about excellence in preaching in the emerging world. They know that they need to keep fresh in their message preparation. They know that in a world like ours, the congregation needs to hear messages from various points of view. And they know they must develop other preacher-teachers in obedience to the principle of 2 Timothy 2:2: "And the things you have heard me say in the presence of many witnesses entrust to reliable men who will also be qualified to teach others."

Pastors of larger churches know that in time they will need to be replaced. What better way to begin preparing than by introducing the congregation to a variety of preachers? North Coast Church in Vista, California, (www.north-coastchurch.com) uses a team of teaching pastors. Senior pastor Larry Osborne does about 60 percent of the weekend teaching, while the other teaching pastors are regularly used. This group of teaching pastors works out the overall yearly preaching themes and then takes on various passages and topics within the series. This allows each teacher to play to his or her strengths.

North Coast has over twenty-one worship teams and no full-time staff person labeled as worship leader. The music leadership for each service is assigned by a part-time person who helps equip, train, and guide the various worship teams. In North Coast's case, these worship teams are usually small ensembles, but there is no reason why growing churches couldn't develop multiple worship teams to deploy not only within the church's regular worship services but also into the community for a variety of services.

In some cases, North Coast even uses a team approach to message preparation and presentation. In planning meetings, various pastors work together to develop preaching series and share insights about the Scripture passages involved. This helps the rest of the team design worship experiences that are pleasing to God while clearly communicating his particular word for the congregation.

Community Christian Church in Naperville, Illinois, is a young church with a young staff (see www.communitychristian.org). The primary directional leader/senior pastor is Dave Ferguson, but Dave is only one of several teaching pastors. In fact, he will tell you that he is accountable to the primary teaching pastor for his preaching. This church offers worship at multiple locations, and each location has a different teaching pastor on any given weekend. The messages are prepared together and customized for each teacher. Each week, a different teaching pastor has responsibility for the direction, but it all comes together through the work of the teaching pastor. (Note: You will see in Chapter 4 that there's a role for a campus pastor that is not necessarily a teaching pastor.)

The lead team at Community Christian demonstrates one of the most mature team-based leadership approaches we have seen to date. Bill was interviewing and videotaping four of the team members while writing this book.[2] We asked them what they considered to be *the keys to "teammanship."*

Jon Ferguson, Dave's brother and community pastor at Community Christian, said, "It has to do with being a confident leader. It's people who love being 'role' players—they understand their unique contributions to the team. It's also having a passion for winning the game more than taking the winning shot. That is, you have to have people who don't care who gets the credit (or at least know how to hide it if they do), a mutual respect that acknowledges each member's strengths, a conviction that God has brought this team together for a particular place and time, and a firm belief that we are individually much less effective without each other."

> **It's about having a passion for winning the game more than taking the winning shot.**

Eric Bramlett, Community Christian's theater arts director, said, "I think the largest single factor is that we're frank with each other in sharing about our own weaknesses and strengths. We can share our struggles and frustrations in a healthy atmosphere. This leads to having much more fun with each other because we're less likely to spend a whole lot of time dwelling on something that we are harboring or are afraid to share. That kind of harboring is what leads to political struggles in leadership.

We avoid those traps because we are so quick to come clean when we screw up and so quick to cheer for each other when we're succeeding.

"I remember the first time I felt as if I were finally 'in.' We were in the field house and planned to show a video. I ended up projecting it onto a wall, and the quality really stunk. When Jon and I went to grab something to eat, I came clean immediately and apologized for the video stinking up the joint. I remember how he praised me for saying it first—the fact that I came clean on it first made it so much easier to deal with and get out of the way. We had a great lunch as a result, without pretending that 'nothing bad happened today...'

"Obviously, this kind of relationship comes from being tight with the vision. You lead by example; in this case, coming clean yourself when things don't come out right or aren't communicated effectively. So since we've developed that good habit, it makes the bad times healthy and leaves much more room for the good times to thrive.

"The more obvious stuff has to do with being very confident in your own area, while staying literate enough in each other's areas to talk about it all. The fact that I don't know much about finance doesn't keep me from having in-depth conversations about budgeting. Nor does it cause our treasurer to devalue my opinion in any way. Jon jokes about being the first creative arts director, but I trust his taste, so I listen when he talks about art. And all of us know small groups."

Some of our readers may be doubting us right now. Perhaps you're wondering, *What about the Holy Spirit speaking through individuals in the act of preaching?*

We believe the New Testament teems with examples in which the Holy Spirit spoke into the lives of the apostles and early church leaders *as a group* and then also through them as individuals. Our modern training (and American individualism) has steered us toward a more individualistic view of the preaching act. But the Holy Spirit can speak to the group in sermon preparation as well.

As the team at Community Christian prepares the weekend messages, it gathers a variety of input from team members, including those who will use the arts to communicate the big idea of the week to the congregation. That input also comes from those who will adapt the message for the small groups, children's ministry, and youth ministries.

When the message text is complete for the week, it goes to each teaching pastor to adapt to his or her own life story and the needs of the particular hearers.

Each teaching pastor adds stories from his or her own life and family in order to personalize the communication.

Some smaller churches with solo pastors use the same idea with sermon-preparation groups. Sometimes these consist of other pastors who meet to share notes. In more cases, teams within the church work on background materials they can submit to the pastor to use in sermon preparation.

These systems for spoken communication can also be applied to the primary worship leaders in a congregation. After all, congregations do need the quality that comes from freshness. They need a variety of styles. That's why worship leaders need to develop other key worship leaders.

In fact, the team approach applies more readily to worship leadership than preaching. Community Presbyterian Church of Danville, California (see www.cpcdanville.org), provides a good example of using worship arts outside of its own church. It has a strong music and worship team whose members have begun to serve not only as worship leaders within its own congregation but also in other churches. The team regularly seeks opportunities in street festivals, fairs, and other gatherings to use a variety of arts to share Christ.

The bottom line in all of our examples is this: In team-based ministry, one primary preacher/teacher does not dominate. Yet sharing the preaching/teaching role is often one of the last changes a lead pastor is willing to make. Nevertheless, sooner or later it has to happen for team-based ministry to be authentic and for the movement to continue to spread.

This is the case because catalyzing a *team vision* must replace simply casting *personal vision*. For movements to spread throughout a decentralized organization, everyone must share in the vision-casting. Even though the leaders we're profiling are incredibly ambitious, their passion for the mission overshadows their need to be the central figure. The primary leader is often the central vision-caster, but he or she ensures that the vision is cast throughout the organization by multiple leaders. In developing their teams, these primary leaders are careful to craft the vision statements not around their personal stories but around the stories of their team leaders and how they are fulfilling the vision.

• **Expand your staff team through internships.** Here is the second of the initial steps you could take in moving toward the Big Three Empowerments. Why not utilize interns? Many of the churches we work with have enlarged their pools of potential staff by doing so.

An intern is a person in training under the direction and care of a more experienced leader. The intern experience has a set time frame, rarely more than two years. It also includes elements of a structured curriculum of reading, reflection, and evaluated practice. Interns may still be in high school, college, or other educational institutions, while others may be much older. They are driven not by educational requirements but by a desire to learn how to do the practical tasks of ministry. We have seen churches with children's interns, youth interns, music interns, pastoral care interns, technical services interns, administrative interns, and so on. We can recall several cases of preaching interns.

In most cases the pay is minimal (if there is any pay at all). Some churches provide housing allowances for their interns. In some cases this is arranged through host homes; in others a church member donates a rental house. One church purchased a small apartment building for use by their interns. No pay, but the rent was free.

A few churches have residency programs for interns. These programs usually focus on a few persons who commit to a two-year course of training and work. They are paid as staff but at a low level. The residency exposes them to a wide variety of training experiences within the church.

At Fellowship Bible Church of Little Rock, Arkansas (see www.fbclr.org), a one-year residency program trains church planters and pastors of large churches. It's designed for recent seminary graduates before they begin ministry at their first church after seminary. The year focuses on personal development as well as skill enhancement related to developing sermon series, church planting, team building, and evangelizing. The residents also participate with the elder board and management team of the church. The Web site of their teaching ministry is www.fellowshipassociates.com. When asked if the residency program benefits the church, Steve Snider, president of Fellowship Associates, their teaching and consulting ministry, replied, "I would say that having five new young men, each of whom are very strong leaders, looking very closely at everything we do as a church—and who are given the freedom to question and offer objective perspectives on our ministries—is very helpful. It challenges us to reconsider how we do things. It keeps us fresh.

"Interns have offered different perspectives and some great ideas related to a number of our ministries over the years. Seeing these young leaders, as they're involved in a number of ministries, becoming a part of our small groups, etc., continually reminds the church of the worldwide impact God has called us to and that we are being allowed to participate in. I think it blesses everybody."

Why don't more churches create intern programs? Two typical reasons are that supervisors don't know how to deal with interns and that supervision takes too much time. It seems to us that the ability to supervise should be expected of all leaders. If a staff person can't supervise, why is he or she on staff? Every paid staff member should be able to design a system of training experiences for interns.

Timeout!

For directional leaders:

- During how many weekends were you the lead teaching pastor last year? Add them up.

- For how many weekends can you realistically teach/preach and maintain excellence? How much better would your teaching/preaching be if you reduced your current schedule?

For congregational leaders:

- Who in your church could assist in communicating the good news of Jesus to your congregation through preaching? Who should be on that team?

- Who in your congregation, other than the senior pastor, should regularly be sharing in the teaching ministry?

Empowerment 2:
Build your board members into an accountable leadership team.

Every church has some sort of governing board. In many cases boards are elected by the congregation and are filled by lay members that serve rotating terms. The members may be called elders, stewards, vestrymen, deacons, or directors, or they may have other titles. Their purpose is to provide directional leadership and governance of the church. While it's true that different systems incorporate slightly different responsibilities and roles, board members are seen as important players in the church system. Some boards are more powerful and influential than others, of course. And boards can be a great help or hindrance to the church, depending on whether or not their members function as a team.

Inside-the-box churches have boards that tend to focus on control and management. Beyond-the-box churches have boards that focus on leadership and accountability. Inside-the-box churches and their leaders usually don't have the board on their team. Beyond-the-box church leaders know that the board is a significant team player within the ministry of the church.

Most outside-the-box churches take a different view. The senior leader gives special attention and time to the selection, training, and development of the board. The board is clearly another part of the total team of the church. Beyond-the-box leaders tend to spend just as much time nurturing their board and the relationships within the board as they do in developing their staffs. These leaders are looking to build teams of staff and board members to move the church forward in its mission.

Most senior church leaders we've observed don't spend enough time in selecting, training, nurturing, and developing the board. Besides the regular board meeting and an occasional conversation with the board chairperson, the pastor spends minimal time with the board. For many denominations in which board members are elected, building the board into a team is difficult. But it can be done.

What are some of the common characteristics of team-based boards? Consider these...

• **They are typically smaller than in-the-box boards.** Since the senior pastor and other staff pastors are spending significant time with these leaders, the group is generally smaller. These groups tend to function as small accountability groups for their members.

• **They meet frequently.** Many will meet almost every week with the senior pastor and other key staff leaders. The meetings are primarily accountability sessions and include time to catch up on the leaders' lives, their families, and their work concerns. Here is an example from Community Presbyterian Church in Danville, California, that indicates the time needed to build this kind of team. Scott Farmer, the senior pastor says, "Our board of eighteen elders and pastoral staff meets from 6:30 to 7:30 a.m. every Tuesday. I open with prayer and ask, 'How have you seen God at work in your personal life or in our ministry together?' We then share stories. Then the preacher for the coming weekend goes through his or her sermon and hears the comments of those gathered. We conclude with prayer for one another and for the church. Monthly, on the first Tuesday, we have our 'business meeting,' which has an agenda based on a two-hour meeting. We also have two in-town retreats a year."

Vision-sharing occurs among all the participants, as well, as they consider some of the core concerns within the congregation. When we observe these meetings, we see board members saying, "Let me follow up on that and take care of it." With this frequent system of meeting, members keep very short accounts. They handle problems and challenges quickly. At times, the pastor doesn't even attend.

In addition to these fellowship times, the board meets in formal business sessions. But because they meet often, everyone on the board knows the various positions of each board member. Conversations about major decisions have usually gone on for weeks both in formal and informal ways. These groups have an understanding of each other and the impact their decisions will have on the church. The board members develop a common vision of the future and know how key decisions will affect that vision.

• **They have more stability.** Inside-the-box churches tend to have shorter, rotating systems of moving leaders on and off the board. This is meant to prevent burnout of board members (and to move individuals off the board who never should have been elected to it).

In many of the beyond-the-box churches with whom we work, even though there is a rotation system, the terms of board membership are longer, typically lasting four to five years in order to provide continuity of leadership. Once a board member is trained and knows the complexities of the church, it's much easier to understand the complex issues he or she will face. One of the key problems with constant turnover is the need to keep bringing all the board members up to speed on issues. (Yet the longer-term board concept is scary to most pastors because they have to give up control and commit to making a team out of their boards.)

• **They require higher commitments to membership.** People are elected or asked to serve because of their prior leadership and their *demonstrated commitment* to the vision and values of the congregation. No one is placed on the board because of "a need to involve this family" or because "their parents were on the board." Instead, these leaders have faithfully proven that they are contributing their time, talent, and treasures to the ongoing work of this congregation.

• **They are included in staff planning, retreats, and meetings.** Wise beyond-the-box leaders treat board members more like unpaid staff than permission withholders. They are invited and encouraged to be a part of the staff-planning processes. Some are assigned to work with various ministry teams. They are invited to come with their spouses to staff retreats and staff meetings. Engaging in all these plans and processes helps board members build trust with the rest of the staff and have confidence in the leadership of the church as a whole.

Timeout!

For directional leaders:

• How would you describe your board? Is it part of the team, or is it that "other" group?

• How much time do you spend empowering your board members to be part of the team?

• Are the people on your board right for team-based ministries? Who is *not* on your board—but should be?

Empowerment 3:
Give lay pastors the power they need for ministry.

The concept of lay pastors takes various forms. In some traditions, lay pastors are credentialed by a central denominational office. These individuals receive a commission to lead congregations when an ordained clergy person isn't available. We applaud this group of ministers, but it is not our focus. In others traditions, certain paid staff who have *not* been credentialed through educational institutions are labeled "lay pastors." They are often effective servants, but they aren't our focus either.

Another approach is to train a few capable individuals to carry out limited pastoral care functions within a congregation. Often these lay pastors serve "in the place of the senior pastor." Although we also applaud this group, again, it is not our focus. Finally, one more method some churches use is to rename all the small-group leaders as "lay pastors." Great! However, there's a beyond-the-box way that also merits consideration.

Our focus here is on *deploying an army of equipped servants within the congregation*. They have different tasks but carry out the same role of leadership by serving the flock to which they are assigned. They could be small-group leaders, care-group leaders, ministry-team leaders, food-bank leaders, or children's ministry leaders, or they may have a whole host of other titles, but their role is to lead and serve the flock. In this scenario, everyone has the potential to be a lay pastor. Understanding this potential makes it possible for all of God's people to realize their place on the team of pastoral leadership both within and beyond the local church. These persons must be encouraged, equipped, and empowered by the top leaders of the church to carry out these roles.[3]

Everyone has the potential to be a lay pastor.

Christ Church United Methodist of Fort Lauderdale, Florida, (see www.christchurchum.org) provides proof that having such lay pastors works, even in the most established congregations. The United Methodist denomination is one of the most hierarchical systems in Protestantism. Yet pastor Dick Wills led Christ Church to abandon the representative type of government in which people are elected to offices in favor of the more biblical model of commissioning lay pastors. In doing so, the church came off a thirty-year decline and has become one of the strongest churches in its region.

The interesting twist to Christ Church is the way people become lay pastors. The only path to receiving this role is by being involved in a ministry as a major leader or by beginning a new ministry. In other words, lay pastors are raised up by virtue of their demonstrated willingness to serve. These lay pastors also make up their church board, which meets once a year for business. During the rest of the year, the lay pastors gather each month to share the stories of what God has done in their ministries. Bill has had the privilege of being in a couple of these gatherings. He says, "If only the rest of my tribe [Bill is United Methodist] could experience this type of a gathering! Then they might be willing to give up their boring, lifeless, and many times hostile, board meetings."

Are You Ready for the Excuses?

Of course, you'll face many challenges on the way to implementing teams. For all of the congregations we've observed, we see very few effective and fruitful teams. For one thing, in order to develop a church with teams, the primary leaders must experience a significant transformation in their Mental Maps regarding the public leadership of the congregation. That is, the senior staff leaders must become willing to share these roles, and the board must be willing to bless and empower this sharing. Leaders must come to accept that all areas of leadership need to be shared, including the most public aspects—preaching, teaching, and leading worship. Such a change will not come easily to leaders who fear losing control!

We're talking about the egos of the senior pastor and the worship leader. Many leaders are more than willing to have a team develop the media or drama portions of their church's worship. But will they take the next step and develop teams for preaching, teaching, and worship? When the answer is no, we hear a variety of explanations, all of which have to do with an ego that is a bit too large. Let's explore these excuses and expose the egos behind them.

Excuse 1: "I am the only one trained to do this." This one usually comes out of the senior pastor's mouth. When you dig deeply into the training of senior pastors, you will find that, at most, the pastor has had two or perhaps three preaching classes. The rest of the training has involved mentoring and on-the-job learning. The fact is that many people within the congregation often have much more training in public speaking. These same persons could work with a team to develop appropriate spoken messages for the congregation.

Excuse 2: "We must keep the quality high in this role." Both the worship leader and the senior pastor have been known to use this excuse. They believe they are the only ones who can deliver the messages in music and word in a way that appeals to seekers. Yet quality actually suffers when worship leaders and teaching pastors aren't fresh. With multiple services each weekend, it's difficult to keep quality high by depending on just one or two leaders in upfront roles.

Excuse 3: "Hey, some people come just to hear me preach." But if people are coming only to hear one person preach, they are limiting the quality of their relationship with Christ. Could we help them move forward in spiritual growth? Do you want to build a church around one personality or around a well-rounded team of teachers/preachers?

Excuse 4: "We have radio and/or television programming that demands a good show." A church needs to ask itself, "Is the broadcast media driving our worship program?" It is always a mistake to let a media audience drive the format for worship. Focus on those who are worshipping in person, not the ones watching or listening in at a distance.

Excuse 5: "Since I cast the congregational vision, I must be the one speaking to that vision each week." Vision has to be cast in all sorts of contexts, not just during a sermon or message. Vision flows from the mouth and life of all the team members—or it isn't vision. It has to be cast in every meeting, every conversation, every written communication. Pastors must be able to take the vision to their key leadership teams. Why? Not so these folks can just repeat it; rather, so that they can begin to fully own it, further shape it, and then extend that vision into their own ministry contexts.

For effective and fruitful teams to develop, primary public leaders must set aside their desire to control how everything happens. They must learn that there's a power in teams that no single individual can ever harness. They must choose their core teams wisely, effectively train their team leaders, and embed the congregational DNA throughout the congregation. Then they can sit back and watch it work.

Equipping leadership teams is a key part of moving beyond the box. Teams are challenging, though. They need strong leadership. Crises and conflicts arise in teams just as they do in other organizations. They are not magic solutions. However, our contention is that the move to teams is the first Mental Map to change in order to move toward getting beyond the box. But there is a second Mental-Map change needed. It involves *equipping* all the ministry roles throughout the whole congregation, which is the subject of our next chapter.

Endnotes

1. Jim Collins, *Good to Great: Why Some Companies Make the Leap...and Others Don't* (New York: HarperCollins Publishers, Inc., 2001), p. 21.
2. To view this video interview, go to www.easumbandy.com/beyondthebox/video/communitychristian.
3. For more on developing leaders throughout the congregation, see Bill Easum's *Leadership on the OtherSide: No Rules, Just Clues* (Nashville: Abingdon Press, 2000).

Chapter 2

Beyond One Team:
Moving to a Culture of Equipping

It was a fairly traditional, medium-sized, African-American church, where the senior pastor had served for over twenty years. At the worship service, several well-dressed persons sat behind the pulpit. Later that week, my interview with the pastor focused on these young men and women.

"So all of those are your associates?" I [Dave] began.

"Yes."

"And only a few of them are paid by the church?"

"That is correct. They all serve in a leadership role, but most make their living in some other way besides ministry for now. Most of them will go on to be full-time pastors at another church in the future, *if* they continue to serve well. Some will never make it."

"So where did you get all of them?"

"All were members of my Pastor's Club."

"Tell me more about that..."

The pastor described his twenty-year approach to mentoring called the Pastor's Club. This club had yielded all the current staff members of the church and had sent at least twenty-five other pastors out to serve other churches. In addition, the club had produced several missionaries in parachurch contexts, along with a number of others who were trained in ministry but now served in government, social service agencies, and educational institutions.

Each year the pastor selected a dozen thirteen- to fifteen-year-olds for membership in the Pastor's Club. He chose them based on his observation of their character and spiritual commitment—and his belief that they had potential for ministry. He took some referrals from other church leaders, but mostly he relied on his own wisdom and judgment.

Throughout the school year, the teens assembled in his office for one hour each week. During the meeting he simply shared a little Scripture and described what it's like to be a pastor. Often his wife joined him to talk about the life of a married couple in ministry. A great deal of personal sharing and storytelling flowed from the pastor.

He regularly told these young people that he felt each of them had potential for very special service to God, though he was unsure what it would involve. He stressed the importance of their actions, not just inside the church but everywhere. He stressed personal discipline and purity that they might be vessels fit for service well into the future. In a sense, these initial meetings were exploratory in nature. The club really had no stated purpose at that point, so the youths attending did so because their pastor asked them to and their parents encouraged them to go.

Eventually the pastor would say to them, "We are going to learn together about some of what it takes to be a minister during this year." He would point to several of them: "You two are going to meet here next Monday and go with me to do some hospital visitation. You three will meet my wife and go with her and some of the ladies to the homeless shelter. You three will report to Deacon Jones on the same night to sit in the back during the finance committee meeting."

And he continued until all of them had an assignment. On the following Wednesday, the group would meet and talk about what they had observed. The rotation continued through several practical phases of church life for a number of weeks.

Then the pastor told the group, "The next thing we will learn is how to construct a talk." And so he walked them through his method of assembling a sermon. For this task, he invited them to come around his desk and see the materials he used and observe how he made an outline and how he jotted his notes. In his case, he talked about constructing succinct phrases that his hearers could remember. He stressed the importance of preaching and that it is a central task of the church. After that he told them the themes and Scriptures that he was going to use one month from that date. Their homework was to construct a talk on those themes during the coming month.

Each week they would return with their outlines. He would comment and correct them. He would suggest a book or another resource...and off they would go to continue their work.

When the next month came, he would tell them the sermons he would preach—and the sermons *they* would preach. Usually four or five of the students would make the cut for the weekend services, and the others would be used during the midweek service. On the weekend services, these youngsters would precede him in the pulpit, and then he would preach a sermon complementing the young preachers' themes and texts. This was done both to affirm the young person and to show the young person how the expert would handle the text.

In all the cases, the pastor would be there with them during the sermon, leading the amens and the applause. And he would be there afterward to put his hand on their shoulders and say, "Well done."

In the weeks that followed, he would make assignments for the young leaders in training to lead the children's service, the youth service, the nursing home service, and a variety of other more public opportunities for speaking and leading. Each week they would report back on what had happened and ask questions about things that had confused them or about how to address certain situations.

As the summer approached, several of the young people were asked to help in the summer-long day camp with more experienced workers. Others were invited to assume servant roles in the larger ministry of the church.

As the group members aged, the pastor continued to track their progress on a more one-to-one basis since he had already started the next year's Pastor's Club, essentially repeating the process each year. Over time, he selected some of the members to be interns in specific ministries and some for part-time staff roles. He selected others to work at another church during the summer that they might "help out our friends." In all cases, he gave them weeks to report back on their experiences.

Some of the club members were directed to higher education, and, often with church-generated scholarships, they were encouraged to continue ministry-specific training. Others went into fields such as education, social work, politics, and the law. The pastor would help them form their vocational plans with the goal of including a ministry component.

And what was the final bit of teaching the pastor always gave his club members? It was the most important presentation of all: "How to run a Pastor's Club."

Those who completed their studies well—and continued to serve in the church, community, and kingdom—were invited to become associate pastors. Some eventually joined the paid staff of the church, but most did not. However, over the years, the church always had plenty of leaders who were formed, trained, and coached by this pastor.

When the pastor retires, where do you think this congregation will find its new senior pastor?

Timeout!

For directional leaders:

• What if you had a Pastor's Club? What if each pastor/ministry director in your church had a club of young people? What would be the kingdom impact of this kind of equipping for ministry?

At a time when many churches are beginning to value strong centralized leadership at the top, beyond-the-box churches are developing leaders at every level. In-the-box leaders focus on identifying and discipling a core few but not the whole congregation. Beyond-the-box leaders seek to develop a core group *as well as the entire congregation*. Within-the-box leaders focus on advanced education for a few select staff. Beyond-the-box leaders create development experiences at multiple levels. In other words, they are developing a culture of equipping.

> *The culture of equipping is a wave of the future as well as a blast from the past.*

It's true that some outside-the-box churches have a series of teams that are effective in carrying out the mission of their congregations. Their emphasis is on the value of team-building. However, beyond-the-box churches have teams of servants throughout their churches and have adopted what we call the "equipping mind-set" and are modeling "the culture of equipping." They stress the value of equipping *everyone* in the congregation to serve, whether on or off teams. All persons in the church have, at their core, the call to equip others in ministry. So our premise in this chapter is that beyond-the-box churches create cultures in which all believers are actively involved in equipping and encouraging one another in this mission with God. The task involves two movements: adopting a mind-set and modeling an ongoing process.

Adopting the Equipping Mind-Set

It all begins in the mind. The old Mental Map envisioned a country parish where a priest was the paid holy man and the parishioners cheered or jeered at him. This Mental Map morphed into the farmer-preacher image, which essentially had the same modus operandi. The movement of mass populations to the cities brought much of that mind-set into larger churches that continued to develop a specialized class system in which clergy did the work while others cheered them on.

Our point is that a renewed, more biblical mind-set is at hand! If we are to adopt it, we must begin changing not only how we think but also how we speak. Here are two ways to start:

Begin changing the *language* of organization.

Words create worlds. The language we use creates images and interpretations in our own minds. Our language also conveys to others certain impressions and cues leading to conclusions that may not be what we intend. In any case, one way to examine, assess, and change the culture of any organization is to change the language. Applied to the church, we find that two words hinder the development of a culture of equipping: *staff* and *volunteer*. Today most in-the-box churches have a class system of staff and volunteers (and all the others). We don't like these two terms because all of us were created to be servants of Christ.

So let's first consider the word *staff*. For most churches, *staff person* is the term for one who gets paid in order to serve the church. Most staff have the best of motivations. They are called by God to serve the church at large and, in most cases, a specific church. They love to serve, and they are good at what they do. Some of these staff are part time, and some are full time. Some are pastors, staff directors, assistants, bookkeepers, facilities maintenance persons, and teachers.

It is biblical for some to be paid to serve the church (see 1 Timothy 5:18). We salute these people, and we do not intend to demean their service. The problem is that often *paid staff* comes to mean the people who are the best equipped to do ministry. In some cases they function virtually as hired guns at the beckoning whim of the congregation. They are not there to lead, much less to equip. They've been put in place to take care of the spiritual needs of the people and to maintain the institution. If a person has grown up in an in-the-box church, this is his or her normal view of staff. All of the other members are designated as *lay people*. (We often hear people refer to themselves as *"just a lay person."*) Such a mind-set does not lead to a culture of equipping.

> *Using the word* volunteer—*or referring to* staff *as the primary doers of ministry— radically hinders a culture of equipping.*

However, beyond-the-box churches have a growing number of unpaid staff. These persons carry great responsibilities but are not paid by the church for their service. They serve for the sheer love of serving, and they exemplify the staff of the future. We salute these people and pray that their numbers increase.

Using the word *volunteer* also hinders a culture of equipping. In its pure sense it is not a bad word. It simply refers to doing a task willingly and freely, not under compulsion. In our own country's history, the word connoted a form of military participation in which people served without being compelled to do so.

In our contemporary context, the word has come to refer to a person who can do a certain task *that is not as important as other tasks*. In church language we call this person a slot-filler or warm body. In many churches, these people are seen as the ones who "do the little things." We know that no church can function without these servants, and we affirm them. However, to view some of God's people as inferior in service to others just isn't biblical. And it clearly hinders the development of a culture of equipping.

> *Many in-the-box pastors we have interviewed state a recurring problem: "We don't have enough volunteers." What they actually mean is that they don't have enough Sunday school teachers, greeters, parking lot attendants, nursery workers, small-group leaders, youth counselors, band members, offering counters, vacation Bible school workers, welcome-center attendants, and a host of other roles that tend to go unfilled at times.*
>
> *Everyone knows that these roles and servants are vital to the growth and health of a local congregation. Every church needs them. So pastors constantly ask us, "Do you know of*

a class, system, or methodology that can assure we'll always have enough volunteers?"

We enjoy working with many churches that have good systems, classes, and methods to recruit, assess, train, and place "volunteers." They are good, healthy churches, but they still don't have enough volunteers.

So we want to let you in on a secret: Beyond-the-box congregations—which have great systems for equipping, training, and placement—always have ministries that need servants. Jesus said it best: "The harvest is plentiful but the workers are few. Ask the Lord of the harvest, therefore, to send out workers into his harvest field" (Matthew 9:37-38). Christ always needs more workers. That will never change.

If a congregation is constantly adjusting itself to God's direction for its body of believers, that congregation will always need more team members to carry on the work. God will always be stretching them in new ways. If your church needs more volunteers, relax; you're normal. Give up the search for the magic wand to solve your "volunteer problems."

We are seeing more and more leaders adopting the culture of equipping described in Ephesians 4:11-13: "It was [Christ] who gave some to be apostles, some to be prophets, some to be evangelists, and some to be pastors and teachers, to prepare God's people for works of service, so that the body of Christ may be built up until we all reach unity in the faith and in the knowledge of the Son of God and become mature, attaining to the whole measure of the fullness of Christ."

In some cases, leaders have used this passage to justify setting themselves up in one of the roles listed by Paul. They have missed the point of the text. The focus of the text is on the practice of equipping the body of Christ. Most of the New Testament was written as a training manual to equip believers to join God in God's work on earth.

In beyond-the-box churches we never hear the word *volunteer*. It simply isn't part of their culture. Instead, we hear them using terms such as *servant, team member, teammate, worker,* and *leader.* Sure, these terms have their baggage as well, but churches that stay away from the V word have a better chance of developing a culture of equipping.

We feel that we need a new Mental Map that employs a transformed language based on biblical truth. The church doesn't consist of a class of people to serve and others to be served. We are not servants and seekers. We are all servants who sometimes serve and at other times are served. The language of beyond-the-box churches is that everyone is a servant of Christ and his mission. A culture of equipping is possible only after we internalize this Mental Map and begin to model it in all that we do, in every area of the life of the church.

Timeout!

For directional and congregational leaders:

• What words do you use to describe your congregation and your leaders? Do you use the term *servants*?

• Do you embed in your servants the values of what you want to create in the congregation's culture? Talk about any evidence you see.

• How will your Mental Map have to change to make a culture of equipping a reality in your church? (Be as specific and practical as possible.)

Begin changing the *understanding* of leadership roles.

Even though many church leaders are beginning to understand their roles to be equippers of others for service, most of the institutional systems have not caught up to this shift in mind-set. In fact, most churches give little attention to measuring how well leaders equip their team members, and few learning institutions equip the equippers to train others. If they do, they continue to promote a system of interviewing and placement, similar to the methods used within a factory or corporation.

One prominent congregation we know uses a performance-evaluation document with staff members. By God's grace and competent leadership, this church has grown to over five thousand people and is starting other congregations. The church has a large number of persons on staff, and we consider most of them to be effective in their roles. However, their performance evaluation isn't designed around the value of equipping. It uses ten performance factors, seven of which deal with the individual leader's own performance and have little to do with leading others. One performance factor targets "relations to others." Another evaluates "sharing with those outside of the church." The final factor, down at number ten, is a measure of how the leader gains cooperation from others.

In our opinion, this approach to evaluating is totally backward. The number one measure of leaders is not their individual performance, their commitment, their knowledge, or their personal leadership. Rather, it is their effectiveness in equipping others. This is true for all leaders, whether paid or unpaid.

Equipping for service must be the prime value of the organization, and it must be modeled in words, behaviors, actions, and evaluation processes if a culture of equipping is to develop. The great measure of a church resides less in its *drawing* capacity than in its *sending* capacity. The most effective and fruitful churches we know are those with cultures and Mental Maps—not just systems and tools—that lead a follower of Christ into the "fields ripe for harvest," wherever those fields may be.

> *The key measure of a leader in equipping churches is "How effective am I in reproducing myself?"*

Equipping congregations constantly ask, "How effective are we in reproducing ourselves in others?" In other words, the key role of worship pastors is to equip and train others to lead worship. The key role of the youth pastor is to equip and train those who lead youth (this includes the youth themselves). The key role of the setup team leader for the weekend worship service that meets off-site is to equip and train other setup team leaders and servants. The key role of every leader is to equip others to lead. This is true of pastors, of governing board leaders, of all the servants of the church.

Two anecdotes from a great congregation will help us understand how this transformed understanding of leadership roles plays out in everyday church life. We have enjoyed visiting New Hope Christian Fellowship, Oahu, on several occasions. One of our key learnings has come from Dan Shima, one of the senior pastors there. Dan has often told us the "pick up buckets" story, and one Sunday we witnessed the event live. But first he asked us a setup question: "What's the most important thing in the church service?" Dan asked.

Like most respondents, we ventured, "The message?"

"No."

"The music?"

"No."

"The welcome and greetings?"

"No. But you're getting closer," he said. With a gleam in his eye, he continued. "I will tell you. It's the offering."

He laughed before continuing, "Most preachers understand this. So what do we do to involve a new person right at the beginning? We ask them to help with the offering. Like most things we do, it's not difficult. Suppose I'm an ordinary member of the congregation. I say to a friend whom I've brought to the service, 'I need you to help me today with my ministry here.'

"The friend will say that he doesn't know how to do anything or doesn't think he's qualified. But I tell him it's easy: 'All you have to do is pick up buckets.'"

Dan then explained the bucket story to us...

"You see, when we first started, all we had were these paper painter's buckets for the offering. We just handed them out down the row, and people passed them along. So there are two jobs for the offering—pass out buckets, pick up buckets."

One Sunday morning we watched two people carrying paper buckets down the side aisles of the auditorium while one of the pastors was talking about the offering. One person was holding the buckets while the other person was giving hand signals about where to walk and how to take the top bucket and pass it to the first person. A hand waved across a mouth followed by a smile reminded the other person to smile.

A few seconds later, buckets were passed down to the end of the row where the new person—and when I checked, a first-time guest—was picking them up, stacking them inside each other, and carrying them to the back of the auditorium to hand to another person.

Later in the week, we asked Dan whether what we had seen was an application of his story.

"Oh, yes, I know her," Dan replied. "And it was also one of our newer members who got her first-time-visitor friend to help. The member was originally reached through the bucket ministry. Then she brought her friend to the church for the first time that morning. She asked her friend to help her with her ministry, so she did. It's just not that difficult to pick up buckets."

"How long has the newer member been attending?" we asked.

"I don't know, maybe a month. She came with another friend who asked her to help with the offering on her first visit, and the friend trained her to do it. Now her first friend serves in another one of our frontline ministries. The offering is one of our initial types of ministries. Most people move on to more challenging things fairly quickly. Oh, by the way, I think the friend who helped the new member on Sunday prayed to receive Christ during that same service."

Here's another story along the same lines: In the same service at New Hope, they showed a brief video titled *New Hope in Action*. Such brief video segments usually feature one of the servant ministries as well as communicate some upcoming events or opportunities to the gathered congregation. On this particular Sunday, the focus was on the parking lot attendants at a new satellite lot across the busy highway from the high school where the church meets. The video showed a dozen people dressed in orange safety vests, smiling, waving at cars, hugging people, and shouting...

"It's fun to help people get to church on time."

"It's so easy to serve people in this way, and lots of fun, too."

"We have a great time out here. We keep a cooler of water bottles in case we get hot."

"We're always looking for other people to join our team."

At the end of the video, an interviewer asked one of the people, "How did you get involved with the parking lot team?"

"I came with my friend to church," she replied. "We attended the earliest service, and then I helped him during the next service with parking cars. It gave me a chance to meet lots of people here at New Hope."

These kinds of statements carry multiple messages that communicate fun, servanthood, fellowship, and the satisfaction of involvement. What can we learn about a beyond-the-box understanding of leadership roles from the example of New Hope Fellowship? Consider a few general principles regarding service and roles that flow from their experience:

• **Service roles are simple.** Pick up buckets, wave cars this way, and smile. The tasks can be easily explained to anyone and easily attempted with little or no training. The point is that everyone needs a simple way to begin serving. Christ himself exemplified this in his simple acts of servanthood toward his own followers (see, for instance, John 13:1-17).

• **Service can precede salvation.** The invitation to service often precedes the invitation to a relationship with Christ (and often is extended on or before a visit to the church). People bring their friends and say, "Come help me." This is radically different from hearing a general announcement from an unknown member (or pastor) who urges them to "come help the church."

• **Servants bring servants.** The servants are recruited (and often trained and mentored) by other servants, personally and quickly. That way, the tasks are accomplished with a friend close by. It's all about friends involving friends.

• **Roles are visible, thus important.** Other visitors, who did not come with friends, see everyday people serving. This is critical! (By the way, do the servants, especially first-timers, sometimes mess up? Sure, but these things can be corrected quickly when a friend is close by to help.)

• **Roles make simple tasks fun.** Service should not be drudgery, no matter how hard the task. Part of the fun is doing the tasks with a team. Another part of it is providing an atmosphere that encourages the servants to enjoy their tasks in the midst of accomplishing them.

• **Roles are modeled more than "taught."** This form of equipping doesn't require curriculum or a series of classes to attend. It only requires leaders who live what they teach. It is the "Jesus way" of equipping.

Timeout!

For directional and congregational leaders:

• List some of the simple tasks that need to be done in your congregation. How can these be designed for fun and involvement?

• How can you help the servants and leaders to develop the mind-set of inviting newcomers into ministry?

• What process do you have in place to encourage every leader to combine modeling with academics?

Modeling the Equipping Culture

The call to model a culture of equipping is the biggest challenge to our existing Mental Maps and one of the hardest parts of getting beyond the box. We live in a culture defined by academic degrees and accomplishments. Although there's nothing inherently wrong with education, our culture has taught us to believe that we should use traditional training models to equip people for their roles in the body of Christ. We challenge this belief. Modeling is much more powerful than cognitive approaches that focus on education and knowledge acquisition.

What can you do to change the situation? We'd like to suggest at least four simple things you can begin practicing immediately.

1. Think "army," "athlete," and "apprentice."

Let's start by going back to the Bible for our most basic premises and images. For example, the imagery the Apostle Paul employs is extremely useful and informs a beyond-the-box approach to equipping. He gives one of his young pastors some powerful clues that will help us. In 2 Timothy 2, Paul tells Timothy to consider himself an *athlete* and a *soldier*. We also know that Timothy was in a kind of pastoral *apprenticeship* with his experienced mentor. So let's look at each of these images, in turn, to see how they can be applied today.

> *Think training more than academics.*

Chris was a recent high school graduate who lacked a clear sense of direction in her life. So she joined the military to see a little of the world and develop some skills. The first thing the Air Force did was make her exercise. They got her body in shape. They gave her a few instructions on how and when to salute an officer, just enough to keep from getting into real trouble. But she received few answers to the "why" questions that swirled around the boot camp trainees' minds. The Air Force believed in teaching behaviors first. Chris would have plenty of time later to learn the whys and wherefores of service.

Similarly, in advanced military tactical training, leaders stress carrying out the proven tactics for success in the field. When a unit is conducting an operation, success depends on previous training in similar situations. Therefore, units undergo numerous training exercises in varying contexts and scenarios. After each action, the soldiers are evaluated in an "After Action Review" to help them analyze their performance and uncover areas that need improvement. Such training helps unit members make decisions quickly and effectively in future assignments.

Likewise, when any athlete begins a sport, very little time goes into understanding the mental aspects of the game. The emphasis is on training the body to perform the required skills. Anyone who has ever observed a T-ball game played by five-year-olds understands this. The players are arranged on the field and told their positions. Numerous coaches on the field tell players what to do with the ball when it comes to them. At first, none of the players knows why they are supposed to throw the ball to first base. Then they are confused as to why they should throw it to the pitcher. And the batter who hits the ball off the tee has to be told where to run and when to stop.

Over the course of the season, though, the lights begin to go on in the youngsters' minds, and they begin behaving in the accepted ways of the game. They begin to make the throws to first base, and the first baseman learns to catch it and touch the base. They begin to watch their base coaches when running. They learn how to call "time" at the top of their voices. It will still take a few seasons before they understand the whys of the sport, but they at least achieve a fundamental understanding of *how to behave* to bring success to their team.

After all, it's impossible to explain the intricacies of baseball on the chalkboard. The same is true for the training of servant leaders: It is impossible to explain servanthood on a chalkboard. Seeing it modeled—and doing it—is the place to begin.

We're not against academics. We both hold multiple degrees and teach in some of the best educational institutions from time to time. We value the knowledge and tools gained in those contexts. But without practical training, knowledge is not useful.

We've looked at the soldier and athlete as biblical models. Now let's talk about the apprentice. We might begin by asking, How, then, is this culture of equipping applied in a practical church context? It happens through apprenticeship.

The most common example of the apprentice model comes through in the role of small-group leader within a church. Most churches have some form of small-group system to assist believers in personal nurture and spiritual growth. Some of these systems are called Sunday school classes, some are home groups, some are neighborhood congregations, and some are ministry team small groups.

But regardless of the name, the key to sustaining, growing, and multiplying these groups is the training of leaders. And the most effective method of training, we believe, uses the apprentice model. In this case an apprentice leader, and often a future apprentice, is always identified when a group starts. The upfront expectation is that one day the apprentice will lead a small group (regardless of whether he or she ever does). This person is given encouragement, training, and opportunities along the way to exercise leadership within the group.

At the selected time, this person then chooses another apprentice to go with him or her to start a new group or team. The apprentice track may include a class on effective leadership, but the key training comes through observation and interaction with an existing leader. This is an example of one-to-one equipping. And get this: You can do it with every role in the church.

We love what Wayne Cordeiro, senior pastor of New Hope Christian Fellowship in Oahu, says on this topic: "The first time, I do, and you watch. The second time, we do together. The third time, you do, and I applaud."

Timeout!

For directional and congregational leaders:

• How many apprentices/interns are in your system? If this area is weak, what can you do to encourage all of your staff and leaders to be more intentional about mentoring?

• How intentional are you in role modeling the importance of apprentices/interns and holding others accountable for the development of apprentices/interns?

2. Build a sweet spirit of respect.

Bill once took a group of church planters to New Hope to spend three days with pastor Wayne Cordeiro and staff. At one of the sessions, a church planter asked how New Hope fostered such a wonderful spirit throughout all levels of the congregation.

The group was amazed at the story Wayne told. In the first year of New Hope's life, during one of the long, early Saturday morning setups for Sunday morning worship, one of the servants (they call them Levites) snapped at another servant. It wasn't much of a snap, no vulgarism; he just let an unpleasant tone coarsen his words. Pastor Wayne overheard the comment and called the man aside. He told the man that such treatment of another servant wasn't part of New Hope's culture; he should go home until he got himself together. He could come back next week. The man begged to stay, but Wayne wouldn't allow him to.

The group could hardly believe that Wayne took that kind of action over such a minor incident. When asked why he was so hard on the man, Wayne replied, "You asked how we foster such a sweet spirit at New Hope. That's how. You must take care of the little things before they become big things." We could see the light bulbs go on in the church planters' heads. Large-scale conflict doesn't happen overnight. It's allowed to grow and blossom as we ignore the simple things such as courtesy and respect.

Anyone who has been to New Hope and talked with any of its servants has experienced a warmth and genuine concern rarely found in any congregation. Such a spirit didn't just happen; it has been modeled by everyone, including the senior pastor.

Timeout!

For directional and congregational leaders:

- When confronted with an angry or out-of-sorts person, how do you typically respond?
- What first steps could you take to begin encouraging a culture in which people deepen their mutual respect?

3. Deploy "seekers" and "day-olds" *now.*

We've already seen that a church such as New Hope can deploy non-Christians into simple service ministries so they catch the value and emphasis on servanthood before they even know it.

> *Here are the two key questions to ask in determining the presence of a culture of equipping: (1) Can it be done by everyone in the church, for everyone in the church? (2) Is it so much of a value that everyone sees it as a fundamental part of being a believer in this place?*

Allen Jackson, senior pastor at World Outreach Church in Murfreesboro, Tennessee, (see www.wochurch.org) stunned us with his answer to one of our questions last year. We asked him to share some of the measures his church uses to evaluate success. He answered that he uses this crucial question: "How many service roles in our church and community have we created for day-old Christians?"

He observed that in many churches new believers are not adequately discipled because they are not serving. So World Outreach made a strong effort in the previous year to identify ways to involve brand-new followers of Christ in ministry. (At the time, this church had grown by over five hundred new attendees over the previous twelve months.) Many of the opportunities they identified served the community at large and not the local church.

Allen continued, "We learned a lot from Steve Sjogren's ideas on servant evangelism [see www.kindness.com]. With very little instruction and direction, people can create great service ministries to share the love of Christ with nonbelievers and develop servant hearts at the same time. Hundreds of churches are now adapting the idea of servant evangelism to create easy-to-understand and -apply methods for day-old, month-old, and years-old followers to serve others and share Christ."

In almost every community organization, new members expect to serve. Many became involved in those organizations because they were asked to serve *before* they were asked to join. Most churches have reversed this process. But why?

> *How many ways can you identify for day-old Christians to serve? Can such a plan be part of your discipleship of new believers?*

Timeout!

For directional and congregational leaders:

• List the servant ministries you have for first-time guests, day-old Christians, maturing Christians, and spiritual giants.

4. Encourage intergenerational servanthood.

One of my [Dave's] top-ten churches in America is the First Baptist Church of Leesburg, Florida. It is one of the most creative churches in ministering to its community and excellently models intergenerational ministry.

62

During one of my visits, I walked into the children's shelter, which takes in young children for emergency foster care. It was around 4:30 on a bright spring afternoon. Over in one corner were a teenager and a senior adult playing a game with a group of children. On the couch were another teenager and an older lady holding some children in their laps while they watched a video. In the kitchen, two teenagers and two senior adults were preparing dinner. In another area, a teenager and an older adult were folding sheets that had just come out of the dryer.

I interviewed several of the servants that day. When I asked why they were there, their responses were pretty consistent: "We are the hands and feet of Christ in this community. We're just acting out his love in a practical way to these children." This was a fairly stock answer, so I assumed it was trained into the servants around that church. If that is so, it's pretty great. But I pressed the question with some of them. One older lady said, "To tell you the truth, I like being around these young people; they inspire me," as she waved her hand in the direction of some of the teenagers.

I asked a teenager the same question. The girl said, "Of course I enjoy giving love to the children, but I really like hanging out with some of these older people. They listen to me and are interested in me and my life. They give me courage for the future."

We think that these teams are extending Christ's love to those children. But also it is being built up and encouraged within those teams. The teams serve not only out of love for their work but out of their love for each other. The modeling of service is taking place between the generations.

* * * *

We began this section of the chapter by contrasting society's emphasis on academic training methods with the more biblical modeling approach. Sadly, most church leaders have bought into the educational training philosophy. The church has become quite successful at setting up training classes that transmit ideas and principles from one person to another. As leaders, we often believe that education will lead to understanding, which will result in behavioral change. Sometimes behavioral change does result. But church leaders have vastly underplayed the value of modeling the behaviors, principles, and mind-sets they seek.

We're aware that some very effective churches do not share our view. These churches believe that every servant in their congregation should be adequately discipled through an intentional process, then trained in ministry, and only then deployed into a ministry that fits their gifts, passions, and talents. The most effective practitioners of this model have good systems that rely on cognitive, classlike, or small-group systems to carefully explain their values with heavy doses of Scripture, personal counseling, and explanations of the church's values. In some extreme cases, this is a three-year process that precedes a person's deployment into ministry.

We applaud any success that arises from such methods. But our point is this: While some form of cognitive training is essential, *if that is all that's being done, then it's only half of what's necessary.* Both cognitive training *and* modeling make for a culture of equipping.

> *Modeling is much more powerful than cognitive approaches that focus only on education and understanding. Combine them for powerful effect!*

Timeout!

For directional leaders:

- Describe in writing how you intentionally model disciple-making.

- How many of your congregational leaders model such behavior?

- What can you do to improve the modeling among your paid and unpaid staff?

What have we learned about the key characteristics of a culture of equipping? Here are eight basic principles that can help you evaluate your church's culture and show you where it can go.

• **We all must become servants and equippers.** Both practices are a natural and essential part of following Christ. Therefore, a church is wise to look for ways to create easy avenues for friends to involve friends in ministry as well as create simple and visible ministries for day-old believers.

- **Every leader must be an equipper—and should be evaluated in that role.** Whatever model of discipleship the church is using—such as spiritual gifts, teams, and/or small groups—the equipping is done around that model. In the case of pastors, they should be the equippers of other leaders. They should not be doing ministry alone. If they are, they are doing it wrong. Equipping is a key ingredient in any biblical form of leadership.

- **A culture of equipping requires apprentice leaders to be involved in one-to-one and group contexts.** A church can't grow the culture of equipping beyond its ability to raise up teachable apprentices. As a result, many of the leaders we studied have started a "farm" system. They view everyone in their church, beginning at a very young age, as potential leaders. One church we studied used the small-group system as early as the first grade with the purpose of teaching leadership.

- **Start them as young as you can, but don't be afraid of teenagers and older folks.** True, you can show young children how to minister to others. (The most effective children's programs we've seen not only reflect great inspiration and imagination, but also include service programs in which children observe adults in ministry and then serve alongside their parents and other adults.) Many churches place an emphasis on service with teenagers, but they tend to focus on isolated mission trips and not a continual servant ministry. Teenagers need to be on the servant teams within the congregation. In addition, old dogs can learn new tricks, if you will model for them and set high expectations.

- **Modeling doesn't depend on size.** We've noticed that the earlier the modeling is done in the life of a church, the more productive it is. This practice should be built into the culture of the congregation from the start.

- **Modeling focuses on learning, deployment, and reflection.** It is best when people are taught, modeled for, deployed, and then brought back to discuss what they saw, learned, and did. This form of equipping is the way Jesus discipled his twelve apostles.

- **Modeling costs almost nothing.** Time is the big investment, not money. Several times a year, one pastor and his wife hosted parties in their home for the young people as well as the "graduates" of the program. Their cost came mainly in time, energy, and involvement.

- **Modeling pays huge dividends for the kingdom.** When modeling occurs throughout a congregation, everyone—from the nursery to the seniors—

experiences affirmation and sees love in action. The church gains a cadre of potential ministers, and the kingdom gains trained servants.

Why don't more churches use modeling? For one thing, it's countercultural. We have at least a two-tiered or three-tiered Mental Map of how to "do" church. To see everyone as a servant and equipper of others doesn't fit our current Mental Maps, our training institutions, or the normal ways of doing church. Most long-term church people think the church comprises "deciders," "doers," and "those to be served." Churches commission certain people to make the decisions and look for people who will carry out those decisions. It is rare for long-term church members to even think of themselves as servants. Instead, they are likelier to think of themselves as "those to be served."

Another reason church leaders don't model is that it's uncontrollable to a large degree. It's linked to vision and values rather than who is in ministry. Because control has been drummed into many leaders' heads and hearts, many times the control value wins out over the equipping value.

As it is with all forms of change, it's easier to start with new people rather than people who cling to old Mental Maps. If your church is having a hard time attracting new people, perhaps it's time to cast your net on the other side. Maybe it's time to reach out into the community around you with the good news. That is the theme of Part 2.

Part 2
Ministry Beyond the Box

Now that you've explored what it means to approach *leadership* beyond the box, it's time to focus on *ministry* beyond the box. Here we'll look at three exciting movements of our time—and invite you to join them. Chapter 3 delves into the various streams of the church-in-a-city movement. Chapter 4 examines the joys and challenges of multisite implementation, and Chapter 5 takes you right to the heart of the church-planting movement.

The leaders and congregations you'll get to know in this section should encourage and inspire you with a brand-new vision. Since these churches function more as movements than as institutions, their goals reach far beyond just growing the local church. *Are you ready to catch their kingdom passion and vision?*

> *These leaders simply weren't willing to base their ministries on geography or architectural space. They were attempting to solve a kingdom-growth challenge rather than a local-congregation challenge. That's why they focus on people and mission. They leave the rest to God.*

Chapter 3

Beyond My Church:

Thinking Kingdom Community

We've just finished reading a fine biography of a contemporary political leader. This man grew up in a small, rural community in Alabama. Everything in that community revolved around two congregations. Even though these churches represented different denominations, the members worked together to improve their community. They had great influence because the congregations were small and based upon personal relationships. The culture of those churches flourished amid proximity ("we live close together"), economic necessity ("we are all poor sharecroppers"), and a small circle of relationships. They all knew one another and their families.

Those simple days are just about over, aren't they?

Most North Americans now live in more urban locations. Our cities have become highly stratified, complex networks of relationships. Although a group of people may be living within the same community, many layers of racial, ethnic, economic, educational, and lifestyle differences tend to keep them separated. It is impossible to know everyone anymore.

As a result, *our communities aren't likely to be changed by any single congregation or leader.* Instead, they will change only as God's people band together, not around a common table but around the common mission of being the body of Christ in every corner of our communities. We believe we are seeing the first fruit of such a body. And it has been given a name: church in a city.

Tomorrow's Trend: The Church in a City

Many inside-the-box leaders still cling to notions of effective ministry that flow from previous generations. Our in-the-box culture has defined a church pastor and leader's ministry as serving just one church. But isn't that the wrong image and a false role? Even though a particular congregation may be one's calling, it is never the whole of his or her ministry. It may even be the smaller part of the ministry. In our view, the trends of the future call us to think and act beyond just one church. We believe God is calling church leaders to adopt a church-in-a-city Mental Map.

If this calling outranks a calling to a single congregation, so that the congregation sees itself as a subsection of a larger kingdom entity, then just about every behavior and practice of that congregation changes. When a church views its ministry as a larger part of a whole within a community, yet still knows its specific vision in relation to other kingdom churches, then the time, talents, and treasures of that congregation turn 180 degrees. But that's not all. Such a view of the church will not only change the way our local congregations function, but it will also change the way the unbelieving world thinks about the church.

Let's spend a little time expanding upon the contrasts. You see, at a time when many church leaders are beginning to think outside the box and catch the vision for their congregations and ministries, beyond-the-box churches are thinking beyond their churches and serving the larger kingdom communities in their areas. Inside-the-box churches focus on institutional survival and keeping the church doors open. They have a mentality of scarcity, dependence, and, in many cases, resentment of other ministries in their community. Outside-the-box leaders have moved to a level of appreciation of other ministries and leaders within their community. But beyond-the-box leaders and churches move to enlarge the entire kingdom within their geographic area by proactively encouraging the other kingdom-focused ministries to transform their communities for God.

Inside-the-box leaders spend the majority of their time thinking about what happens on Sunday and during the week at their local congregations. They are consumed with the details of their own small systems. They think of the congregation they serve as "my church" and focus their thinking and discussion on that congregation. Their question is "How do we get things done in my church?"

Outside-the-box leaders know better, in many ways. While they focus more on large-picture issues, most of their concerns still revolve around their particular congregations. Their question is "How can our church do great things?"

"How can the churches and the people of God transform this community?"

Beyond-the-box leaders have a different approach. Their mental pictures include not only their churches but also other similar churches in their community. Their view of kingdom ministry includes other churches and organizations that have an impact on that particular mission field. Their question is "How can the churches and the people of God transform this community?"

Leaders act according to how they answer the preceding questions. Inside-the-box church leaders focus all their energies on solving problems within their particular congregations. Outside-the-box leaders figure out ways their churches can make an impact but act as if God is relying on *their* churches exclusively to get the job done. Beyond-the-box leaders go about networking and using the kingdom resources throughout the community to accomplish God's purposes. They bring other kingdom leaders into a process that attempts to view the community from God's perspective. They help develop each part of the body's response to what God is doing in that community.

My Church—or Beyond?

Consider the stark contrasts between the two approaches...

My Church	Beyond My Church
Place	Territory
Operations	Opportunities
Traditions	Strategies
Internal focus	Outward focus

Our purpose in this chapter, then, is to describe how some of the beyond-the-box leaders are working with kingdom partners from other churches and organizations to develop innovative, healthy ministries for their larger communities. This movement has several streams to it, and even though they are all headed in the same direction, we find some truly distinctive tributaries. After all, who could ever harness the creativity of the Holy Spirit? None of these movements is perfect, though each is helping to pioneer a new way of seeing the church and approaching ministry.

We will share some examples and principles from these streams. We'll also attempt to explain the pastor/leader's roles in these movements. Our purpose is not to do an in-depth study of these movements but rather to encourage you to explore them and begin participating in them.

No Big Surprise?

Let's pause here to consider what exactly produced this kingdom movement. Practitioners with a church-in-a-city Mental Map are being shaped by a variety of factors. Those with a historical bent will say it's a return to the early church when, for example, Paul addressed his letters to the entire community of believers in a city, not just to a particular congregation. Others would say the movement is a genuine visitation of God upon a city or region that is ripe for it.

We do not discount these factors. However, God seems to have set the stage for church in a city through several other factors, too. Therefore, it's hardly surprising to us that the time for it is just right. Here are eight of the contributing trends we see.

1. The decline of the church's influence in the community—All the religious leaders in this movement seem to know that the religious community isn't the vital voice and presence it once was. They have heard the tales of a previous generation, or of other communities, and they genuinely long for the day when, once again, the church will have a strong voice and influence in the community.

2. The decreasing attraction of denominationalism—Most denominations have fallen on hard times since the 1960s. The denominational background of a congregation now makes little difference to the general public. Almost every mainline denomination is declining in numbers and organizational strength. Localism and self-determination have triumphed, and most congregations couldn't care less what happens in their judicatory and national body. It just isn't relevant to them and the ongoing work of their churches.

3. The failures and/or successes of the previous generation of ecumenism—The ecumenical movement tended to focus on establishing organizations and bodies that attempted to "speak for the churches" in a city or region. These bodies often became debating societies for controversial issues rather than transformers of the city. Most are now struggling for redefinition because the life has left them. Some would label this decline as failure. Other commentators claim that these organizations were a great success. They erased many of the lines between churches so that, in many cases, clergy can serve churches of multiple denominations. Some of these councils of churches found some common-ground projects that rallied congregations to a cause. Either way you see it, the old ecumenical movement plowed ground for the emergence of the church in a city.

4. The rise of strong parachurch movements—While the ecumenical movement and denominational groups technically could be called parachurch movements, we are referring to the thousands of independent groups around the country that minister without the benefit of a particular church. Since many parachurch leaders eventually become pastors, they are already used to working with numerous churches in their communities. They are driven by a "way of doing church" that transcends the boundaries of a purely local entity.

5. The importance of Christian media conglomerates—Over the past few decades, many companies, radio stations, magazines, and book publishers have developed products and services to serve markets larger than any particular tradition or denomination. They have an economic interest in building the largest set of buyers they can. Through Christian radio and TV, for instance, listeners and viewers get a variety of perspectives on the church. The same can be said of Christian publishing. It is garnering a broad market that has grown at a rapid pace for almost thirty years, untethered by denominationalism.

6. The growth of, and general openness to, the charismatic movement—This movement is a part of most denominations in North America. These churches have grown large, and their leaders are prominent in communities. With many of these leaders dominating Christian media, acceptance of their churches has grown. In many cases their emphasis on the Spirit has attracted people from other traditions—mainline and evangelical—and their teachings on being open to the Spirit have influenced the leaders of the other churches.

7. The increasing popularity of independent evangelical churches— Much like the charismatic movement, independent churches that have no denominational or other affiliation are growing and gaining widespread acceptance. Many have roots in a particular heritage but aren't tied to it. Legitimacy in the community has not been derived by their heritage or denominational ties but rather by their effectiveness in serving the community.

8. The loneliness of pastors—The movement provides ways for pastors to find friendship, accountability, encouragement, and real help with their leadership issues. Imagine the interaction and sharing! This helps explain why so many pastors will devote many hours to serving and participating in these movements while ignoring the official business and committee meetings of their denominations.

Timeout!

For directional leaders:

• What vision are you casting for the kingdom in your area?

• What is your church's part of that vision?

• How does your church's part of that vision influence the relationship with other kingdom leaders?

For congregational leaders:

• Does your church have a God-sized vision for its community? What is your evidence, pro or con?

• Suppose God were to move powerfully and the vision for your church were suddenly fulfilled? What would that mean for your church?

• How would your church's practices have to change in order to respond to God's mighty work?

Ready for Some Real-Life Examples?

Now it's time to see how the church in a city looks in real life. Some of the churches in the following examples have been influenced by books, others by groups and movements. Still others have developed indigenously from their sense of God's call and their recognition of the needs of their communities. But in every case we've seen, when leaders sense a call to the church in a city, the way they do ministry radically changes. That's the main point.

As we've said, you'll find various streams in this movement. Here are three examples:

The Valley Vision: Spreading the Blessings

The Valley Vision refers to a group of fifteen churches working together in the San Ramon Valley east of Oakland, California. This section of the Bay area has a population of a hundred thousand. Several years ago a group of pastors there began to meet and pray together. They were aware of the reconciliation movement, popularized by Promise Keepers, and it influenced their thinking as well as the pastor's prayer movement and the church-in-the-city movement in Colorado Springs.

The members of this group began praying and talking about their mutual vision for God's work in the valley. By studying their churches and other churches in the valley and comparing the attendance and membership to the total population, they determined that approximately 15 percent of the valley's residents were somehow related to a church. As a result, the group began to ask God to pour out his Spirit in such a way that they would see that percentage double before 2007. Specifically, the Valley Vision prayer is "Lord, would you allow us to be a catalyst to double the percentage of people in this valley who confess Jesus Christ as Savior and Lord, connect with a Christian church, and contribute to your cause with their lives?" The shorthand way they say it is "Confess, connect, and contribute."

They felt three things were necessary to reach this goal: (1) All of their churches must change in order to grow. (2) They would have to plant new churches to reach new people in that valley. (3) They would have to begin sharing all of their resources among the fifteen churches.

Scott Farmer is the lead pastor at Community Presbyterian Church (CPC) in Danville, California, a large PCUSA congregation with a long history in the heart of this valley. Scott has been involved with the Valley Vision leadership team from the beginning of his ministry. He has helped the staff, elders, and entire congregation of CPC get their heads and hearts around the Valley Vision. Reviewing the changes this one church had to accomplish in order to make the Valley Vision viable will help us better understand what is involved in being part of such a movement.

• **They considered the impact of success.** What if God moved in a powerful way to double the number of believers in a short period of time? How would that change the congregation's ministry? Would the congregation be ready for the result?

• **They decided to spread the blessing.** They embedded in their hearts the truth that the blessings God had given CPC were not their own; those blessings were meant to be shared with others. This sharing would include their budget, their staff, and their facilities. This Mental-Map change is huge. CPC can no longer act unilaterally to reach the valley but must walk in partnership with the Valley Vision churches in every way possible. They have reallocated their budget to honor the Valley Vision. Among other reallocations, they are now helping fund a student ministry in an Assemblies of God church. Two other churches, a Foursquare and an Independent congregation, are also helping to fund that ministry. Even the "Deacons Fund," a CPC account set aside for community needs, has now been broadened to help other congregations meet needs they uncover within the community.

• **They transformed the staff roles.** Job descriptions changed to include allocating staff time to serving other churches in addition to the CPC congregation. Along with seeking to grow CPC, the staff now must be concerned about the growth and health of the other valley congregations. For example, one of their worship leaders was assigned to help a Baptist church that was without a worship leader. And since they are one of the larger churches, their staff at CPC is helping to gather and convene other ministry leaders in youth, children's ministry, worship, and other areas to help coordinate ministry in their valley.

• **They revamped their promotions approach.** No longer does every outreach effort come packaged with the CPC name and information. Some outreach activities have been labeled "sponsored by a consortium of Valley churches" rather than carrying the label of just one church.

Amazing, isn't it? Could your church make these kinds of changes? Would the people be ready for the blessings the changes would bring to the entire region? As you consider it, let's travel to Texas...

The Church in Houston:
Transforming the Pastoral Vision

Mission Houston is a movement of leaders and churches whose mission is "to serve the whole body of Christ as it mobilizes for the purpose of the ongoing transformation of the greater Houston area." Jim Herrington serves as one of the leaders of the movement. The members of this leadership team began to meet and pray with each other around the dream of a transformed city.[1]

With this goal in mind, the movement has gathered several hundred churches and leaders. In order to get a handle on an area as large and sprawling as Houston, they divided the city into natural geographic communities. Each of these is served by a facilitator who helps gather the leaders in praying, strategizing, and discerning how God is at work in their community.

For those in the city-reaching stream, the goal is to reach functional unity among the pastoral leaders and then develop a common map of the "harvest field" and "harvest force." The harvest field is a diagnostic map of the area that includes real data on spiritual, physical, emotional, social, and other needs. This map includes information on topographics, demographics, pyschographics, and other systemic issues that face a community (such as occult activity, crime, drug and alcohol abuse, and other behaviors that drain the spiritual life from a community). The harvest-force map shows the churches and other ministries that serve the harvest field. This map examines the various ministries, their strengths and needs, and their potential focus areas.

The components of the unified church (as represented by the leaders of those congregations and of the sectors of the city represented in those congregations—such as business, education, law enforcement, health care, and social services) are brought together with the two information maps to a "congress" to discern God's vision and purpose for the area church. The process leads the gathered group to commit to a clear understanding of priorities, goals, and activities that will transform the area.

All the churches don't work on the same priorities. Instead, they focus on a common map so that each knows what role in the body it is playing within that harvest field. Some projects are undertaken jointly. Some work is done cooperatively, such as the planting of ten new churches in a specific area with the Baptists doing some of the work, the Methodists doing some, a large independent church doing some—all with shared information about target groups and successes.

These processes take time—time to build relationships, to heal old wounds, to clarify motivations and intentions, to pray together, to ask God for fresh vision, and to map areas of needs and strengths. The practitioners of this approach stress the need for a strategic view of the area—and a view of the entire process—before proceeding to tactics.

No single congregation dominates or leads the process. True, certain influential churches are quite large and have highly visible leaders, but these leaders and churches take up the role of servant in order to better facilitate the work of the entire church in the city. An example of this kind of servanthood is found in the Katy Church (the name given to the several congregations working together in the Houston suburb of Katy). Jim says that he knew there had been a change in thinking when the pastoral leaders in that area began to describe themselves like this: "I'm an associate pastor of the Katy Church, and I lead a congregation that meets at 748 Central Street." In other words, many of the leaders describe themselves first as servants of the Katy Church and second as leaders of a local congregation.

In Jim's view, pastors who are deeply committed to city-reaching "participate regularly with other pastors in prayer and supportive relationships; actively persevere in communicating the community-transformation principles within their congregations; personally invest and lead their congregations to invest money in community-transformation efforts; and actively collaborate with others to discern, articulate, and implement a shared vision." For most pastors this means a deep, radical change in their Mental Maps. However, when this transformed Mental Map resides in several leaders within a community, it profoundly changes how ministry is accomplished there.

The Nehemiah Project: Reaching Out With Blood, Sweat, and... Money!

In January of 1998, thirty-one pastors of the Little Rock, Arkansas, area met to pray over their city. A much smaller group had been praying together in North Little Rock since 1995. This prayer summit led the group to form an organization known as the Nehemiah Group. Notice a subtle distinction in their vision: "To unite the church in the Greater Little Rock area in prayer, growth, and good works that demonstrate the love of Christ and that prepare the way for revival, spiritual awakening, and spiritual transformation in our community." (See their Web site at www.nehemiah-group.org.)

In addition to the regular pastor prayer cells and summits, the group focused on two projects: a map of the needs of the city and a response project known as ShareFest. The mapping project focused on three priority needs. One of the strategies for addressing these needs was to develop partnerships with local schools. ShareFest is a bridge-building tool that helps to develop the partnerships with the schools.

ShareFest is a "doing good works" project shared by the area churches. During the past three years, over a hundred different churches participated in this event. Some of the results include...

- nine hundred units of blood donated to the Red Cross.[2]

- twenty-six central Arkansas public schools renovated and refurbished with congregational "sweat equity."

- $21,000 given for school uniforms for needy children in three school districts.

- $60,000 given to Black Community Developers, a program for at-risk youths.

- over one hundred community projects with three thousand volunteers.

Each participating church undertakes a significant service project in the community. In addition, the churches together collect coats, food, and a love offering to help not-for-profit community agencies in Little Rock. Primary attention is given to building bridges between the churches and the public schools. The love offering goes to community agencies that address the needs in their study, bless the city in a significant way, have a track record of excellence, and are closely allied with Christian values.

Fellowship Bible Church of Little Rock, by virtue of its size and strength, serves the Nehemiah Group and the ShareFest project by providing staff time, office space, and other resources. This congregation is serving the body of Christ in Little Rock, tangibly supporting the whole church in that community.

Gleaning Principles From a Great Movement

Each church-in-a-city movement illustrates some common principles. Here they are in a nutshell:

- The movements grow from **pre-existing relational networks** of pastoral leaders.

- The leaders are **long-tenured pastors**, having developed long-term trust and significant "relational equity."

- The networks share a **common base of prayer** and personal storytelling, leading to spiritual breakthroughs that enable progress to the next level.

- The leaders and churches **covenant with one another**, often formally signing a pledge to serve one another and lead their congregations to serve one another.

- The local church no longer protects its own turf; instead, congregational resources are seen as **gifts from God to be shared** with the community.

- No one is asked to lay aside denominational distinctives in order to develop common doctrines and worship; rather, churches **focus on the Great Commission task** of transforming the city.

- The leaders have **pioneered the right amount of geography** because the area must be small enough for effective relational nurture and large enough to have an impact.

- The leaders and churches have **a healthy balance of inward and outward** focus, avoiding the breakdown that can happen with a focus on prayer that doesn't move into action.

Pastor, What Will It Mean for You?

We realize the church-in-a-city concept probably challenges your understanding of leadership and the church. But we also know that beyond-the-box churches and leaders are using this Mental Map to change how ministry is done in their areas. The result is growth in the kingdom, blessing to all, and glory to God.

You can be one of these leaders; it simply requires a broadened vision. When thinking about their personal ministries, these leaders begin with the whole city or region in mind. They see that the call of God is to a people in an area, not just to those in one local congregation. This way of thinking radicalizes a church. If we are called, not to serve ourselves but instead our community and the larger kingdom, our entire understanding of ministry changes.

But there's more. The pastor's call is not only to an area but also to *transforming that area for Christ*. That is the driving force behind his or her ministry. Therefore, these leaders seek to find all sorts of projects that further the cause. Almost always this includes church planting as well as community-impact projects such as efforts to improve public education, public housing, and public health. And pastors no longer cringe when a new church is planted down the street from them; instead, they rejoice at having another ally in their campaign of citywide transformation.

Obviously, building relational, prayer, and action networks is vitally important if these pastors want to understand one another. So they spend time together. They participate with other pastors and develop mutually supportive relationships. When another ministry and congregation grows, they rejoice. When one suffers, they all suffer and act to help however they can—and their help is welcomed. They come to care about the other pastors and ministries as much as they care about their own congregations.

Yet because they do lead local congregations, these pastoral leaders regularly communicate the vision to their people and work to adjust priorities, staffing, budgets, and calendars to fit a kingdom Mental Map and ministry. They know that it is one thing to talk about these issues with other pastors in a community and another thing to drive the talk into action at the congregation level. Therefore, in order to accelerate that change, many of the movements have a "saturation church planting" component through which several congregations have this Mental Map embedded into their DNA from the beginning.

Could denominational executives learn from these leaders? Just as pastors are learning that the harvest is truly larger than any single congregation can handle, might overseeing officials begin to realize the benefits of loosening their grip on the denominational turf? Suppose they, too, were to join the rest of the body in the larger vision of fulfilling the Great Commission?

Time to Take the Next Steps

Over the past five or six years, we have observed the church-in-a-city movement springing up in many U.S. cities and making rapid advances. One may be forming in your community. If so, we urge you to check it out. But if not, we recommend you do the following:

Pray. Ask God to change your heart about your own leadership and show you how to serve not only your congregation but also the church in the city. Then ask God for others who would share the vision.

Connect. Find others who share the vision! You'll have to take some risks; rejection and misunderstanding may await you. But you must not short-circuit this process. It takes time and ongoing relational work over an extended period of time. Remember, you are putting together a movement, not a program.

Learn. Get good information. You might begin with the endnotes at the end of each chapter in this book and the resources listed in the Appendix

(p. 140). Check out the books, articles, Web sites, and other groups we've listed. Then broaden your search to find the right resources for your community.

Dream. Ask God for the vision, then cast the vision and seek discernment along with others. Once there is a core team of committed pastors in a community, see the task God is calling you to do. This process of discernment will happen through personal conversations with other leaders, an information-collection process, and times of prayer together.

Act. Prayer and discussion must eventually lead to active obedience. Just as in personal discipleship, the group must move to accomplish God's purposes. No matter how powerful the vision, without action the movement will dry up. Make a start; trust God to carry you forward.

Warning: This Mental Map of kingdom transformation by the church in a city is dangerous. It could change you and your congregation in uncomfortable ways.

Much as the gospel changes the soul.

Endnotes

1. The Church in Houston movement has been served by CitiReach International (www.citireach.org) and its president, Jack Dennison, and by the Sentinel Group (www.sentinelgroup.org) and its president, George Otis, Jr. The City Reaching strategies call the church in the city to reach the whole city with the whole gospel.

2. See Robert Lewis and Rob Wilkins' *The Church of Irresistible Influence* (Grand Rapids: Zondervan Press, 2001) for a complete list of all the good projects.

Chapter 4

Beyond a
Single Location:

One Church in Many Locations

At a time when many churches are beginning to think outside the box by adding worship services to an already crowded Sunday agenda or expanding their worship space or looking for a larger piece of property, beyond-the-box churches are expanding their areas of influence by becoming churches in more than one location. Within the box, church leaders think location; beyond the box, they think mission. These leaders aren't tethered to one place. They are developing the untethered church.

This church meets in many locations but has the same core values, mission, administration, budget, treasury, and staff as a single-site church. As such, it reminds us of the church of the first century that met in homes throughout a city. Instead of relying on a location, the untethered church relies on mission and penetration into many corners of the community. Whereas the church-in-a-city movement relies on a variety of congregations to reach a city together, the movement described in this chapter stresses *one congregation growing in multiple locations.*

Although multiple sites and venues may not be right for everyone, we're convinced their time has come. So many congregations are developing and exploring the multisite option that it would not surprise us if, in twenty-five years, multisite congregations were more the norm than the exception.

The key to understanding the multisite movement is to remember that fulfilling the Great Commission drives these congregations, not a growth strategy. For these congregations, space is never a limitation. Mission, rather than space, determines the agenda. It's not so much that these leaders set out to do multisite ministry; it's just that they are ready and open to the movement of God in the church's life. In other words, they are able to see beyond the box when God says, "Go."

More Than One Way, More Than One Place

Although some common denominators exist in most multisite congregations, we haven't found any cookie-cutter pattern. Instead, we've identified at least seven effective approaches. The key is to consider the type of approach that might work best in your situation.

The Apostle Approach

It's one thing to be the *pastor* of a multisite congregation; it's another to be the *apostle* of a multisite movement. Pastors of multisite congregations are moving out of the role of local church pastor and into the role of apostles whose primary responsibility is to oversee the multiple sites. No longer is the pastor the primary pastor/teacher of any one congregation. We expect to see this trend increasing as more leaders move beyond the box of the local church to embrace a kingdom-movement attitude.

In the beginning, these churches develop a second site, which results in another site, and so on. Over time they often begin to centralize authority into an apostolic leader so that the person can oversee the multiplication of new congregations. At the same time, they decentralize the authority of the "lead pastor/teacher" in the individual congregations.

Community Christian Church in Naperville, Illinois, is a good example (see www.communitychristian.org), with its four congregations in the Naperville area. The North Campus, in Naperville proper, is a fairly recent development and meets in a permanent facility owned by the church. They started South Campus, in Romeoville, before they built their permanent facility. The South Campus meets in a community center twelve miles away and was developed in partnership with a development company. The South Campus and West Campus locations have identical worship services each week. The third campus, started in 2001 in Plainfield, meets in a gated community's clubhouse and primarily reaches older adults. The West Campus, started in 2002 in Montgomery, meets in a church facility that had closed and was given to the church.

All four of the congregations have worship services and small-group meetings built around the same "big idea" each week. The worship teams, teaching teams, and support teams from all the locations take part in a common planning and training session. While each church shares the same big idea of the week,

86

each worship team customizes it to make it relevant to its target community. This culture of the big idea makes it easier to multiply and manage the sites as well as reduce the stress on staff. The staff can easily transfer the large-church culture to the small venues, making the reproducing of multisites more exponential.

> *"The Big Idea is the software that holds the multiple sites together for us."*
> —Dave Ferguson
> Community Christian Church

The church's long-term goal is to have ten campuses, two hundred congregations, and a hundred thousand Christian followers in the western suburbs of Chicago. In addition to that goal, they've begun the NewThing Network (see www.newthing.org). Its purpose is "to reproduce networks of multisite churches relentlessly dedicated to helping people find their way back to God." They are planning four tracks of involvement. An *apprenticing track* is for multisite congregations willing to begin their own multisite network of congregations. As part of this track, they are using Web cam and video conferencing to mentor Jacob's Well, one of their church plants outside Denver, Colorado.

Three other tracks will come online soon: a *coaching track* for congregations wanting to become multisite or who are currently multisite, a *partnership track* for those who wish to partner with the NewThing Network in finances and resources, and a *fellowship track* for those pastors and church planters who want to establish a highly collaborative interdependent relationship with CCC and desire to launch a network of multisite congregations.

Community Christian has moved beyond simply being a multisite congregation and is seeking to birth a movement of such congregations. Dave Ferguson, the founding pastor, is no longer the primary teaching pastor or even campus pastor at any location. Instead, he functions in an apostolic capacity. He has authority over the multiple campuses in the Chicago area and over the emerging network of churches, including their church plant (Jacob's Well) in Thornton, Colorado.

> *"The multisite movement is a new thing God is doing. It gives churches desiring to 'help people find their way back to God' a third option. The first option is to grow larger in one location, the second is to start new churches in another location, but the third option is to grow larger in multiple locations. The multisite strategy is the preferred option for most growing churches. Multisite strategies reach more people faster, with higher quality, greater results, and lower costs."*
> —Dave Ferguson

When asked what he would tell other churches wanting to be part of the multiple-site movement, Dave offered the following seven steps:

Step 1: God-thing. Be clear that God is at work.

Step 2: Vision. Be sure the vision comes as a result of God being at work.

Step 3: Leader. Commission the right person as the campus pastor ("face with the place").

Step 4: Team. Add the right staff that will help that new campus and the whole church. Also fill the new campus matrix with the right lay leaders, those who are spiritual entrepreneurs.

Step 5: Systems. Make sure everything you do is reproducible, high quality, and in alignment with the vision and goals.

Step 6: Finances. Thoroughly analyze the funding.

Step 7: Resolve. Be unstoppable. As the leader, you must have an unwavering resolve to do whatever must be done.

Another church exemplifying the apostle approach is New Life Christian Fellowship, which has six locations in the Chesapeake, Virginia, area (see www.newlife.cc). Although all six congregations are tied together as one church, with one mission and the same core values, each congregation has its own lead pastor. New Life Christian Fellowship is as much a church-planting movement as it is a multiple-site movement. Each lead pastor is empowered and encouraged to develop new teams to plant new congregations. The intent is to develop a cluster of stronger congregations helping to establish new congregations.

The senior pastor, Bobby Hill, is transitioning into the role of general overseer of the movement. Hill is now the International Director of Vanguard Ministries, an umbrella network that includes the New Life churches. When asked whether he would recommend this approach to anyone else, Hill replied, "I would try to talk them out of this approach. It is right for our church in our context, but it isn't the approach for everyone. This idea is more about the *multiplication mentality* than the form it takes. This particular form just works for us in our region."

The Vanguard movement considers the Tidewater area to be a natural place for planting the sites. But it also feels it should plant independent churches outside of that area. The value of multiplication finds expression in different ways in different settings.

Timeout!

For directional leaders:

- To what extent does your church have a multiplication mentality? How is that mentality expressed in various ways?

For congregational leaders:

- How could your church begin accelerating a multiplication mentality? What first step could you take?

The Video Venue Approach

As we move further into a world that accepts video as a major form of communication and entertainment, congregations are finding that teaching by video is not only acceptable but also often preferable to live presentations. North Coast Church of Vista, California, has two locations but multiple venues (see www.northcoastchurch.com). What makes this approach unique is that beyond having two locations, it has thirteen worship services, ten of which use a video venue, including the off-site location.

Only three of their on-site worship services have live teaching. The worship (music) is live, but the preaching, by video feed, consists of a message delivered by one of three rotating pastors—the lead pastor, Larry Osborne, who preaches 70 percent of the time, and two other members of the teaching team. They've used this approach since the church was very small. Seventy percent of the worshipping members now choose to attend the video venues instead of the live teaching! The video venues, each with various names and styles, are now a part of the design plans for a new facility. For more information on how to establish a video café, go to www.videocafes.org.

> *"Ambiance and worship style are never neutral. They either help or hinder our ability to reach people with the message of Christ. The problem has always been that what reaches one person repels another. The use of multiple worship venues has become a powerful tool for reaching people we could have never reached with a one-size-fits-all style of ministry. I believe that in an increasingly mosaic culture, the ability to offer a variety of worship styles surrounding a common message is no longer an option for growth; it's becoming a necessity."*
> —Larry Osborne
> North Coast Church

Don't confuse the video venue with a video overflow room. The former is not an optional worship service. Each one has live worship and a live host, but the teaching comes via video. During the teaching time, attendees view a full-screen video of the message by whichever member of the teaching team is teaching that week. However, video is only a part of the attraction at North Coast. The total environment is what draws people.

The video venue is an excellent approach for all sizes of churches to expand the scope of their ministries but especially for small churches with few paid staff members and limited space and resources.

North Point Community Church uses a similar idea in a different way. It is located about thirty miles north of the target community of Buckhead, the hot area for upscale living in Atlanta (see www.northpoint.org). But both communities have a similar demography. A group of laypeople from North Point had a heart for the area of Buckhead in Atlanta. The new Buckhead Church meets in a hotel in the heart of Buckhead on Sunday evenings. It uses a videotape of the morning messages from North Point but does everything else live. To this they add a system of small groups. In less than a year, they have moved to two services and now lease a former grocery store.

> *"There are two things I love about the multiple video/venue approach. First, it allows multiple options in styles and times of services. Second, and more important, it allows the large church to feel smaller. The truth is, pastors are the only people who like huge services. Members put up with the large size because of the teaching, programs, and ministry opportunities offered. If they could find those things in a smaller church, no doubt they would be there, in my view...We intend to grow through the multiplication of smaller venues on our campus."*
> —Rick Warren, Saddleback Church

The Rent Approach

As more and more churches face factors that hinder the construction of new churches—such as zoning restrictions, environmental requirements, and escalating land prices—more churches are experimenting with using only rented facilities and never owning property.

Evergreen Community Church in the Twin Cities was started in 1988 by two young non-seminary trained pastors, Mark Darling and Brent Knox (see www.evergreencc.com). Now the church has five congregations. None of the congregations owns space, but their total attendance has reached 3,300. When asked why they prefer rented space, the pastors said, "It's less expensive; it allows us to spend more on leadership development. We want our people's lives and ministries to evolve around their homes and small groups rather than a church building. In addition, renting allows us to develop more sites than if we owned property. And since our mission primarily targets young adults in the urban areas of the Twin Cities, the property isn't available anyway."

Evergreen Community Church represents many of the new postmodern congregations. Its use of rented facilities allows it to be mobile as well as less institutional and building-centered. Their newest location, the Urban Refuge, is designed to reach multiculturals and multiethnics.

"First, Evergreen is called to plant churches; hence, 'many locations.' Second, we are dedicated to the plurality of leadership. There is strength in plurality. The longer strong leadership teams can be together, with leaders sharpening each other, the better their ministry will be. A 'one church, many locations' concept keeps leaders together. Third, there are many efficiencies. Locations can share the same office and office staff. Locations can share the creative talent of creative arts people. Dramas and videos have traveled from location to location. Pastors have even helped one another with their messages. Fourth, each location feels it's a part of something bigger. We regularly schedule events, leadership training, and conferences together. It makes for an exciting time, with a big crowd. We also do new location plants together. It is easy to feel a part of something bigger."
—Brent Knox, Evergreen Community Church

However, some changes are in the wind at Evergreen. Due to some problems with one of the schools they rent, they are considering renting a church building in order to meet their capacity needs. This illustrates again the need to be flexible. These folks are "facilities agnostic" in order to serve the mission of the church rather than be tied to a space, whether rented or owned.

The Apartment Approach

Many beyond-the-box congregations are more concerned with changing their cities than with growing their churches. Therefore, they form alliances with anyone in the city, regardless of denominational affiliation, in their efforts to reach the city for Christ.

First Baptist Church of Arlington, Texas, began Mission Arlington in 1986 to provide Bible studies in apartment communities (see www.missionarlington.org). The importance of meeting people's physical and emotional needs, as well as spiritual needs, became immediately apparent.

In this approach, lay Christians from across denominational boundaries gather people for Bible studies in apartment clubhouses, mobile homes, and neighborhoods. The result is 247 locations with approximately 3,700 people in weekly attendance. This allows specialized congregations to meet the needs of many micro-niches based on culture and social need. The ultimate goal is to provide an opportunity for every person in the city of Arlington and Metroplex to hear and respond to the gospel of Jesus Christ.

A Mainline Approach

Although all of the examples so far have involved independent or evangelical congregations, multisite ministry isn't limited to these groups. Mainline congregations are beginning to develop multisites, although most of them would not consider themselves part of a movement. Perhaps this is because of their strong ties to a denomination. The goal of these congregations usually centers on expanding their mission, reaching a different demographic, or dealing with a landlocked situation.

St. Luke's United Methodist Church in Indianapolis, Indiana, is one of the more liberal congregations to be involved in multisites (see www.stlukes-umc.com). St. Luke's has about three thousand people attending worship each weekend in its ten different worship services. The lead pastor is Kent Millard. Linda McCoy is the pastor of The Garden (see www.the-garden.org), referred to as a "blossom" of St. Luke's United Methodist.

The Garden meets at the Beef & Boards Theater four miles from the primary location. Started in 1995, The Garden now reaches more than eight hundred people in three services each Sunday. The Garden's worship is casual, upbeat, and held around tables and food. Sixty-five percent of the people worshipping at The Garden were disconnected from church before becoming involved. At present, the income and expenses, while administered together, are accounted for separately. Soon The Garden will be expanding to a second site to handle the demand for space.

A twist on the same idea comes from another mainline congregation, Bethlehem Lutheran Church of Minneapolis, where Chris Nelson is the senior pastor. This church was doing a good job of reaching young families. They had grown from seven hundred to twelve hundred in weekly worship attendance in the past few years, but they realized they weren't reaching the younger crowd.

After careful study and reflection, the church called a pastor and musician, commissioning them to start a new expression of the church known as Spirit Garage (see spiritgarage.org). Spirit Garage is a separate congregation that meets in a theater but utilizes Bethlehem for some of its office space and small-group meetings. Pam Fickenscher is the founding pastor of Spirit Garage.

The Spirit Garage leadership has the operational and creative freedom to develop whatever is necessary for the ministry to thrive. Whereas The Garden tends to reach a broad age base, the Spirit Garage laser-targets a certain demographic profile. Its target audience includes those from the uptown neighborhood where it is located—full of urban singles, coffeehouses, and theaters.

A few years ago, Upper Arlington Lutheran Church, in Columbus, Ohio, was prevented by the city from expanding its original site (see www.ualc.org). A lesser church would have rolled over and played dead. Instead, the church purchased a thirty-four–acre site in partnership with a major development company two miles away and built a second campus. The entire congregation is now known as UALC with two locations. They use multiple teaching and preaching pastors across the various services, with all four of their pastors preaching regularly at both campuses. All the pastors use the same text and themes. However, leaders use multiple worship styles at both campuses.

A Small Church Approach

Contrary to popular opinion, multisite ministry isn't just a large-church luxury. We found many examples of multisite congregations with around four hundred in worship and a couple of examples with under two hundred. For example, First United Methodist Church in Sedalia, Missouri, developed a second location when it had only 195 in worship (see www.firstsayyes.com). After existing for 112 years in the same location, this church was landlocked, it had no off-street parking, it was accessible only by stairs, and it was air-conditioned only in the sanctuary.

In 1998, First Church embraced the idea of two campuses and soon became United Methodism's first multisite ministry in Missouri. With the opening of their Celebration Center on Thirty-Second Street in April of 1999, the congregation ventured out in faith. Today they have an average of 436 people worshipping each week. They are best known for their permission-giving systems and attitudes that invite people to say yes—to life, to love, to God. Jim Downing Jr. is their pastor.

> "You hear a lot of folks talk about thinking outside the box. Our ministry is built on the question 'What box?' In fact, this question hangs on the wall opposite my desk, and I look at it every morning. It reminds me that, too often, I have put God, ministry, or life in an unnecessary box. We can do all things through Christ; with God's help, we will."
> —Jim Downing Jr.
> First United Methodist
> Sedalia, Missouri

The Strong Church, Weak Church Approach

Although this approach has been used successfully in more than one location in several denominations, it has the least effective and consistent track record of all the options we surveyed. Still, it deserves mention because of the increasing number of weak congregations in North America.

In this approach the healthy church takes a very strong leadership position over the hurting congregation, often taking it over rather than forming a partnership. When a dominant congregation gives leadership in the new location, the future success tends to be much better than when a weaker congregation still attempts to lead itself. The healthy church provides the staff and program for the hurting congregation and eventually absorbs the weaker church.

Lord of Life Lutheran Church in Fairfax, Virginia, is an example of a strong church helping a fellow church of the same denomination (see www.lordoflife-lutheran.com). The leaders approached their judicatory about the possibility of taking the struggling Holy Spirit Lutheran Church, in Centreville, under their wing. The venture has proven so successful that the congregation is now in conversation with an Episcopal congregation to plant a church together and develop individual and joint ministries.

Timeout!

For directional and congregational leaders:

• Which of the preceding approaches would work the best in your situation?

• What obstacles (other than money) do you see?

• What first steps seem doable at this point?

What Are the Ingredients Here?

Amid this variety of unique multisite approaches, we found several common ingredients that seemed to make the situations work. Perhaps they could be added to the mix that is your own particular ministry situation...

1. They see themselves as "one church in multiple locations." They're not separate congregations. To accomplish this unity, these congregations have a clear, consistently articulated and embedded DNA throughout all the leadership. It doesn't seem to matter who preaches at which location. Dave Ferguson at Community Christian says, "One of the reasons we can easily reproduce multiple sites is our use of the Big Idea. Everyone, at all of the locations, plays off the same page. This makes it easier for our artists to produce worship material for all of the sites."

2. They view ministry as less strategy than response. Most multisite congregations don't set out to be multisite; they set out to solve the problem of how best to accomplish the Great Commission. Their passion for conversion and mission forced them to discover new ways to expand their influence. North Coast Church is a prime example. With five hundred people worshipping in each of its four services and a desire to provide seats for spiritual window-shoppers, this church started using a video feed of the teaching to create a new experience. The video venue wasn't a planned strategy. It was something they stumbled upon in their efforts to find innovative ways around a space problem. Now it is an integral part of their strategy.

3. They see effectiveness flowing from internal leadership development. Most of the pastors came from within the church, and most previously worked in the marketplace, with no seminary training. These congregations develop a farm system for the purpose of raising up new leaders who become the pastors of the multisites. In the case of Evergreen, personal mentoring by each of the multisite pastors is built into the job descriptions.

4. They build on strengths rather than weaknesses. While the initial approach of these congregations may have been introduced to solve a particular growth problem or issue, the solution developed into a new plan of its own rather than remaining a response to a specific situation. The successful congregation then combined its various strengths to build its multisite approach. Often the primary strength may not be planned, as in the case of the video venue at North Coast Church.

5. They function best with team-based ministry. The DNA of the church is so firmly embedded in its leaders that the entire paid and unpaid staff function almost as one, allowing for enormous amounts of flexibility. Community Christian has developed such deep levels of team-based leadership at most levels that the lead pastor is not the primary teaching pastor at any one location. Dave Ferguson believes that leadership development and development of artists are at the core of multisite ministry. He includes artists because the reproducing of quality worship in all the new sites is crucial. Thus, the church even has a school for the arts. The Evergreen Church was started by two young pastors who have served as co-pastors from the beginning.

6. They've dropped the one-size-fits-all mentality. Multisite churches have a passion for offering choices so they can reach different generations and cultures. In some cases the primary target is different attitudes; in others it is different age groups. Evergreen's The Rock targets young adults exclusively. North Coast targets adults with different attitudes, likes, and styles. One video venue offers Starbucks, another Krispy Kreme doughnuts, and another Mountain Dew. The Edge draws those who prefer loud music. Traditions draws an audience that prefers piano and hymns. Each one of these services appeals to a different culture.

7. They form innovative partnerships. One of the growing trends among multisite congregations (and other innovative types) is the formation of partnerships with nonprofit and for-profit groups. Bruno Bottarelli, founder of Marquette Companies, a for-profit real estate company in the Chicago area, began his walk with Christ as a result of attending Community Christian Church in Naperville, Illinois. Over time, he became concerned about the quality of life in the communities he was developing. According to Bottarelli, "We're building beautiful places, but we can't get people to live together beautifully." So a partnership was formed between Community Christian and Marquette Companies.

This partnership resulted in the formation of the nonprofit Institute for Community (IFC), of which Dave is the president (see www.instituteforcommunity.org). The mission of the IFC is "to help people build quality relationships where they live and work through the power of genuine community." The goal is to set a new standard for how communities are developed. A church will be at the heart of every new community developed by the partnership.

Their pilot project is the HighPoint Community in Romeoville, Illinois. At the heart of the HighPoint Community is a community center managed by the IFC staff. Friendship Center houses all the IFC programs and is the home of the south campus of Community Christian Church. It is the epicenter of community in that neighborhood. They are currently considering about a half dozen follow-up projects, including locations in Spokane, Baltimore, and West Palm Beach.

Another church setting the pace in forming partnerships is Eastern Star Baptist Church in Indianapolis. Among its three campuses, it has formed forty community partnerships.

What Are the Advantages?

Beyond-the-box-congregations don't do things just to be doing them. So what *benefits* do they see in multisite ministry? Here are just a few:

The kingdom continues to expand even though the church building is landlocked. In many cases, the land to build new church facilities isn't available. But why build one large building or have all the worshippers in one location?

Options remain open. It can be threatening to longtime members to hear talk about relocating. Adding a second site lets those tied to the building remain while others venture out to the new site.

More non-Christians attend. Multisites are responsible for more converts than relocations. In the case of Sedalia Church, 60 percent of its new members are new believers.

The resources are enormous. Multisites have the benefit of an experienced lead pastor; a competent staff; an established financial base; and a high quality of worship, discipleship, and ministry *from the beginning*.

The larger-than-life mission is inspiring to all. In established congregations, the older generations again feel the excitement of mission and purpose that can be found only in pioneering new ministries.

Ministries are diverse. A congregation can reach a new age group (usually younger) or different ethnic group. Multisites can also establish a new worshipping congregation based on a style more indigenous to the area.

Better stewardship of funds and resources results. It costs much less for a congregation to develop a second site than for a denomination to plant a new church that may or may not succeed.

The laity is mobilized to a greater degree. Multisites open up many new opportunities for lay ministry and require a congregation to strengthen its efforts to recruit, equip, and deploy lay servants into ministry.

Multisites experience more "open doors" than new congregations. Since the church has already developed relationships within the community, it finds some things to be possible that a new church plant might not. For example, schools, one of the favorite places to begin multisites, often have policies that require churches to either have land or purchase it within a certain period of time. Some require the church to have actual plans for the future facility. Others limit the amount of time a church can use the facilities. Utility companies require credit ratings and deposits on new accounts. Multisite congregations avoid much of this.

Alert: You've Got Challenges!

Although we believe the time is right for multisite ministries and have cited several successful approaches, our research also shows that serious issues must be addressed for this ministry to continue over the long haul. For example, in most established churches, one of the biggest challenges facing the lead pastor is convincing the longtime members that they won't be overlooked and forgotten when the new site becomes a reality. Often this concern turns into hostility as the new site begins to do better than the original site. Since the older generations may blame the lead pastor, he or she must have the ability to stand firm and communicate the need and the vision well enough to gather and keep a solid following of key leaders. One of the ways some churches have addressed this issue is by incorporating the remodeling of the present site with fund raising for the new site.

Staffing may also be a problem. In fact, in every case we've seen, staffing the multisite church is a significant challenge. Whether the same staff is responsible for the ministry at all of the campuses or each campus has its own lead pastor, more staff is required. Some congregations provide a pastor for each campus. Some alternate between the lead pastor and associates. Some have the same person preaching at all locations each week.

In some cases, the same preacher/teacher leads all the services live or through video technology; in others, a team of preacher/teachers serves the various sites. Some teams use basically the same material for each service, while others are on different tracks. The campus pastor may serve as the primary visible leader for the particular congregation meeting at that site but could serve the larger leadership of the church in some other role. In the case of Community Christian, the campus pastor is the host, cheerleader, and emcee, but isn't one of the teachers. The campus pastor is the one in charge of answering newcomers' questions. Community Christian refers to its campus pastors as "the face of the place."

> *"All of our campus pastors are people who came from within our church. And the majority of our campus pastors are people who previously worked in the marketplace with no seminary training."*
> —Dave Ferguson

Many of these congregations have multiple music and arts teams that serve the multiple venues or multisites. A church must determine how many different types of music and arts it can support. Is it a unified arts team, or is it decentralized? Who will help give direction to these teams? Will it be a centralized body, a specific leader, or the campus pastor? In other words, setting up multiple sites and venues requires a shift in thinking that has to be addressed in staff selection. If the staff leaders are not comfortable with the approach, they will attempt to frustrate it.

Multisites also require a higher competency level among all staff than found in most single-site congregations. The core staff must be more like "athletic directors." They aren't just coaches or great athletes. They know how to oversee coaches who run teams. These individuals must be team players, highly flexible and motivated and very focused. They need to effectively answer these questions: "With multiple campuses, how does our staff stay together as a team? How does our team deal with the issues of the whole and the issues of the parts?"

In addition, deciding which staff and volunteers will begin the new site is critical to starting another site. The approach of the new site's ministry will determine which staff and volunteers are needed. Many of the congregations have developed various forms of a leadership team comprising some or all of the pastors of the congregations. Before you start a new site, why not add staff who influence all locations so both the existing campus and the new campus win?

The bottom line is that having multisites can be stressful and demanding for paid staff and key leaders. Much of the stress comes from the inability to touch base with everything and everyone on the weekend. The superstar individual begins to be less effective in this environment and must expand, be able to reproduce his or her influence, or move. One of the key issues is how to keep the synergy of a centralized staff while being able to reach out into the community with a decentralized staff. The only solution here is to embed the DNA in every leader at every level of the congregation.

Often the stress is such that congregations starting out in a multisite approach morph into a new approach. Perimeter Church (PCA) of Duluth, Georgia, (see www.perimeter.org) developed four sites as one congregation, then restructured into the Perimeter Ministries International. This transformation sprang from the complexities of managing ever more divergent congregations and people groups. The new approach grew to twenty-three churches. And now the church is adjusting its approach again by releasing the association and accelerating church-planting efforts from Perimeter Church.

Eastern Star Baptist presently has three locations in and around Indianapolis and has decided that future locations will be church plants that are strongly tied to the "mother church" (see www.easternstarchurch.org). The reason for making this shift is to overcome the stress on the core staff.

When we interviewed the leadership staff at Community Christian, it became apparent to us that four things helped them reduce the amount of stress on the staff team. The *"big idea"* helped with alignment. An emphasis on *coaching* helped develop leadership throughout the teams. The amount of energy poured into *lay empowerment* meant that the congregation relied less on paid staff. And almost as a side comment, one team member said, "It doesn't hurt that we sort of have an *addiction to new stuff.*"

Along with the staffing challenges, multisites require careful attention to solid communication and integration of ministries between the sites, much of which can be accomplished by a seamless technological link between the campuses. Although the staff offices may be spread between the campuses, an integrated computer network, phone network, and other devices can make it seem like one campus to the staff and key workers. In some cases, the unifying factor is the vision and administrative structures in which the various congregations have common offices and staff to service all of the needs of each congregation. In some cases the small-group structure is the approach that unifies the whole congregation. Those using this approach have a lecture-lab design in which the small-group focus is always the same as the weekend focus. The congregation is unified through the small-group structure instead of a common worship event.

Never forget that multisite ministry is less a strategy than a response to Christ's command to go and make disciples of all people. It is not just another program or emphasis du jour. It is a way of life, a way of responding to God's call to be the church. So there is really no formula for beginning other than to pray and to examine why you are in ministry in the first place.

Suppose you were to try it as an experiment? Give another location nine to twelve months. If it isn't attracting people by then, it probably won't. Then consider finding a new location and perhaps developing a new team. When choosing the site, think of the persons you are trying to reach. Consider where they eat, where they play, and what clubs or bars they frequent—and then rent one.

Think big. Think "the untethered church."

Timeout!

For directional and congregational leaders:

• What are your greatest strengths?

• Do multiple sites make sense within the type and scope of your call, location, and demographics? If so, who is your target audience? What needs can you meet in another location that you can't meet where you are?

• Why would you develop a multisite rather than simply plant another church? Do you have the staff and funding to pull it off?

• Is your congregation predisposed to outreach already? Has your leadership already demonstrated an ability to grow a church?

• Is there a good temporary or permanent site available? What could you do right now to start checking into the possibilities?

Chapter 5
Beyond Church Planting:

Planting Churches That Plant Churches

Wayne Cordeiro looked me [Bill] in the eye and made a statement that stuck with me long after our meeting was over. See if it has the same impact on you...

"I have only one lifetime to give to my Master. And when I arrive at heaven's gate, he will ask me how many I brought home with me. He will not ask me how many books I wrote, how big my church building or budget was, or how exciting our prayer meetings were. He's going to ask me how many I brought home. The best way to do that is through multiplying churches that reach those without Christ. Church planting is not an end in itself. It is a means by which we reach more souls. Not only will this reach greater numbers of souls for which Christ died, but it will continue to reach them long after we are gone, and they will be greenhouses for new, emerging leaders. That's our heart's cry!"

At a time when very few churches are beginning to think outside the box by considering planting a church, churches beyond the box are developing church-planting multiplication movements. At a time when denominations are struggling with how to plant a few churches that survive, a growing number of congregations are beginning to function as church-planting movements.

The difference between the two approaches is huge. So please realize that this chapter isn't about how to plant a church or even planting *a* church. It's about the emerging church-planting *multiplication* movement that is springing up all across North America. Most church-planting efforts in the past focused on...planting churches. While we recommend any form of church planting, we believe it's more important and strategic to the kingdom to *focus on planting reproducing churches that will become the centers from which other churches will be planted.*

Do you see the difference? Such congregations may partner and work with denominational church-planting efforts, but they do not let the locus of activity reside there. Unlike most approaches to church planting that are sequential attempts at *addition*, these movements involve the exponential *multiplication* of concurrent efforts.

How does it work? Let's begin by looking at some of the best examples in the country. Every church we'll mention has a track record of reproducing at least four new congregations a year. This is a very high rate of reproduction, going well beyond congregations that plant a church now and then. We hope these examples will inspire and encourage you to move beyond addition to the process of multiplication.

It's All About Planting and Networks

The congregations in this section have an organization, system, and culture in place that result in developing and networking church-planting leaders who are dedicated to starting their own church-planting multiplication movements. Often these organizations work with multiple denominations and groups in establishing new churches in a region. The organizations are extremely flexible and fluid and are always changing to meet the needs of a changing landscape. Planting reproducing churches is embedded in their culture. Their primary goal is not to develop an organization but to plant congregations that become centers of church planting.

The vision for multiple church planting usually flows directly from the founding or lead pastor of the church-planting church. The primary leadership for the planting team comes from the pastor as well. These people establish a team of leaders that own and operate the vision and implementation of a church-planting system. Their assessment systems use formal and informal means to qualify the team leaders. Some of the planters are trained as interns in the mother church, some in a church plant, and some in both. The coaching comes directly from the mother church's designated church-planting coach.

There is often a peer network made up of the leaders of the other plants from that church. The resources often come from a combination of the mother church's funding and the church planter's own fund raising. The core groups may come from the mother church, or the planter may gather new attendees in the target area.

Some of these congregations function as the mother church; some do not. Some train their interns on their sites; some at other plants. Some have systems designed to flow financial resources back through the network of church plants to develop more plants; some do not. But they all have one thing in common: *They plant congregations that become centers for church planting.*

Here's a look at some of these innovative congregations.

NorthWood Church

Since 1992, NorthWood Church, in Keller, Texas, has planted forty-seven churches in the United States alone (see www.northwoodchurch.org). NorthWood helped start its first new church less than three miles from the original site. "I figured that if I was really serious about this kingdom stuff, we needed to start our first church right around us to show we really meant it," says Pastor Bob Roberts.

In time they called Andy Williams to oversee church planting. During the next few years, NorthWood helped start seven churches within the surrounding few miles. They then reached out nationally and globally. The result is that NorthWood has planted nearly fifty churches and in the next eighteen months will have close to seventy-five new daughter, granddaughter, and great-granddaughter churches. So far they are starting about ten new plants a year, most of which are Baptist congregations. Each church NorthWood starts is required to "church the area" and is viewed as a church-planting center both locally and globally. So these new congregations are working "glocally"—with local and global outreach—from day one.

NorthWood's weekly worship attendance is 1,500. But when you count the churches that immediately surround it, that number jumps to 4,000. This does not include the attendance in three other churches—of different denominations—that NorthWood mentored in their early days.

Everything NorthWood Church does grows out of its members' understanding of the kingdom of God, which they believe should be lived out in the context of the local church. The kingdom has to be personalized, not just in the lives of a few called and ordained leaders but throughout the entire congregation. They believe the church is the missionary and that the Great Commission was given to the entire church, not just to professional clerics. Each member is challenged and encouraged to obey Christ's call to make disciples.

> *"I am obsessed with the kingdom. I read everything I can get my hands on.* What does it really mean to practically live it out in the context of the local church? *That's what I want to know."*
> —Bob Roberts
> NorthWood Church

The phrase "Kingdom in, kingdom out" is the hallmark of their preaching and thinking about the church. They live the first part of Matthew (the Sermon on the Mount) in order to fulfill the last part of Matthew (the Great Commission). NorthWood has inseparably linked evangelism and discipleship. If Jesus and his kingdom are primary to one spiritual journey, expanding that kingdom by starting new, vibrant, reproductive communities of faith has to be top priority. By focusing on the Sermon on the Mount, this congregation makes personal transformation the focus and impetus for everything else. That, in turn, leads to church transformation and kingdom expansion. Bob says, "Our call is not to build the largest church in the community. We are called to 'church the community.' That will take lots of churches."

NorthWood prefers a design-focused approach rather than model-focused approach. Each situation calls for the leaders to have on-the-spot design abilities. Thus, the focus is teaching young church planters to think and strategize based on the local micro-culture. NorthWood has helped plant churches that are seeker-, cowboy-, ethnic-, postmodern-, high-modern–, and sending-oriented, among other varieties. Its premise is that all expressions are valid and should be encouraged rather than focusing on an industrialized model where one size fits all.

Under the direction of Andy Williams, NorthWood's Church-Starting Center has developed a comprehensive process for recruiting, assessing, training, developing, deploying, and coaching these leaders. In 2002 alone, NorthWood mentored twenty interns to plant churches. In practical terms, the process looks like this:

• Recruiting. They constantly look for the best and brightest leaders. They believe the key to their movement is selecting the right person for the right job at the right time.

• Assessing. They analyze and assess the strengths and weaknesses of all of their recruits, utilizing several personal profile and behavioral inventories they've developed.

• Training and development. In this area they assist all planters in exploring their call, values, vision, strategies, and team-development abilities. They also teach how to become a sending-based church, immersing the couples and teams in the principles and practices of effective, design-oriented church starting.

• Deployment. Planters get involved in reading and written assignments, in ministry-skills training, and in learning leadership development through one-on-one time with a mentor on the NorthWood staff.

• Coaching. Preparation for deployment isn't complete until ongoing coaching is in place to help with site selection, resource gathering, pre-launch preparation, and launching of the new church. Experienced church-plant coaches maintain monthly contact with church planters and stay in relationship with them. The coach does not consider the job complete until the new church has reproduced and is part of a strategic, regional network. While some church-planting initiatives focus on assessment, and others training, the bottom line for NorthWood is "How many churches actually get off the ground?"

NorthWood's church-planting training includes another key component: teaching church planters how to raise money. Though in some cases North-Wood helps to raise funds for a church start, it mainly finds partners who will supply some startup money. If a potential church planter cannot raise funds for a church plant, then he or she cannot plant a church.

Timeout!

For directional leaders:

Think for a moment...

• How many people are under the influence of Christ because of your church?

• How many people are under the influence of your church because of other churches you have planted within your community?

• How many people are under the influence of your church because of churches that your church has directly planted around the world?

• How many additional fields of ministry do you think are possible as you read and pray?

For congregational leaders:

• What if the mission of your church was changed to reflect not how many people were in your services but rather how many were in churches that your church helped plant?

• How would this mission change the way things are done in your church?

Acts 29

In 1989, David Nicholas, pastor of Spanish River Church (PCA) in Boca Raton, Florida, and Mark Driscoll, pastor of Mars Hill in Seattle, Washington, developed an organization called Acts 29 (see www.a29.org). It's a network that provides training, funding, and friendship to like-minded churches desiring to join God in the planting of church-planting churches. This network had its roots in the multiplying efforts of Spanish River Church, which had been planting at least one church a year for twenty years. In organizing the network, they hired Mark's founding elder and administrative pastor, Eric Brown, to run Acts 29 full time. The network plants mostly postmodern churches, although not through their denomination.

"Acts 29 is the byproduct of God's transforming grace spilling out of his people into all nations of the earth as they live in freedom and joy. Church planting is simply what we call the results of this power of the gospel that has pulled us into its wake."
—Mark Driscoll
    Mars Hill Church

Before applying for assistance from Acts 29, the church planter must gather a core of fifty people who confirm that God has called them and pledge to give of themselves and their monies to the new work. Only then can one apply to Acts 29, and even then the potential planter and members must further pledge to commit themselves to evangelization through the preaching and teaching of the gospel, to walk in holiness before God, to have a male elder lead the church, to become self-funding and self-governing, to begin planting other churches within three years, to give 10 percent of their general funds to other church plants through Acts 29, and to attend an annual boot camp for assessment and training. Here the candidates either put together their launch plan or are told that Acts 29 doesn't feel they are called to this ministry.

The potential planters who appear called, along with their spouses, are invited to an international summit (at no cost to them) so that Acts 29 can see the progress of their work and decide whether or not to fund them. If they are funded, it is for no more than three years. Once accepted, they are invited to an advanced coaching time of fellowship, mutual encouragement, and resourcing with the other network planters and their spouses to help make sure they're ready for their upcoming launch. Acts 29 prefers the planter to have one hundred people in the core group prior to the public launch.

Funding comes from a variety of sources: Spanish River and Mars Hill, the 10 percent gifts from the churches in the Acts 29 network, partnerships with churches outside the network, and donations from individuals and organizations. The unique element here is that the money given by the planting churches does not go into a central pool but is sent to a new church plant determined by the local elders of a funding church. This practice ensures that churches are planting churches and not supporting organizations or networks.

In the same way, the coaching, accountability, funding, and reporting go back to the church and not to some bureaucratic headquarters. Since the monies do not go through one general account, the churches sponsoring the new church plants have a vested interest in praying for and holding the new work accountable; after all, they have directly sacrificed for it. The leaders of Acts 29 feel that church planting is too often done by organizations and denominations rather than churches; therefore, they go out of their way to decentralize their efforts.

New Heights Church

New Heights Church, led by Pastor Matt Hannan (see www.newheights.org), houses and funds Northwest Church Planting (NWCP; see www.churchplanter.com), led by Dave Reynolds. NWCP has assisted in planting approximately twenty congregations, several of which have reproduced in their first three years, which is what they expect to happen. At present, they plan to help plant six to eight more congregations over the next twelve months.

For many of the plants, New Heights doesn't serve as the mother church. Instead, NWCP oversees the movement. NWCP is an interdenominational church-planting movement that pulls together denominations and seminaries for the purpose of planting healthy, reproductive congregations. It has a pipeline of training that involves several entry-point events dedicated to three priorities: drawing, developing, and deploying.

> *"Our passion for planting churches comes from Jesus' words to the Apostle Paul in Acts 26:17b-18: 'I am sending you to them to open their eyes and turn them from darkness to light, and from the power of Satan to God, so that they may receive forgiveness of sins and a place among those who are sanctified by faith in me.' For many people, the church plant is the last exit from the road to hell. We plant churches so that people have every opportunity to turn around and go in a new direction."*
> —Dave Reynolds
>   Northwest Church Planting

They *draw* potential planters from everywhere they can but primarily through their annual Church Planters' Summit, their denominational contacts, their application process for church planters, and their close ties with Multnomah Biblical Seminary. (Pastors from New Heights teach in the seminary, which offers a master of arts with a church-planting emphasis.)

They *develop* these church planters over one- to two-year internships, either at a new church plant or at a planting church. Their goals for these interns are to look, learn, lead, and launch. Candidates go through a four-day discovery process in which seasoned church planters assess each couple's ability and readiness to plant. Those who are accepted train for the pre-launch phase of the upcoming plant. They receive assistance in clarifying and articulating their purpose, vision, values, strategy, structure, and timeline.

Finally, they are *deployed* as resident church planters, as part of a team. The resident church planter is more than an intern. This person has been chosen to go out, when the time is right, to plant a church. Each pastor of each church plant is responsible for constantly raising up two resident church planters. This is one of the ways NWCP ensures the future of the movement. During this time they attend quarterly church planters' forums and attend the Lead Planter Network, a monthly gathering of pre-launch pastors that trains them in fund raising.

Two things about this approach stand out to us. First, the heart of their training is the local church-planting church, which NWCP assists. NWCP feels it could never provide what the environment of a plant provides, so it doesn't try. Instead of functioning as the mother church and having the interns on staff while in training, it pairs potential planters with a new church plant where they do their internship. Working in the new church plants accomplishes three things: It helps staff the new church plant, it helps the new church plant become a mother church that will reproduce, and it helps the potential planter gain firsthand knowledge of what church planting requires.

Second, their goal is to be as localized and decentralized as possible, with multiple training centers. This means multiple networks of loosely connected groups exist in many locales. So far, they have centers in the Seattle and Portland areas and are working on centers in Alaska, central Washington, Spokane, and Phoenix.

NWCP works cooperatively with local churches, seminaries, and various denominations. The congregation uses its own resources to fund the initial training and startup of the new churches without requiring any "payback."

Redeemer Presbyterian Church

Tim Keller, pastor of Redeemer Presbyterian Church, has a long-standing love affair with the city of New York. A comprehensive description of Redeemer's vision, values, and approach to ministry can be found on its Web site, www.redeemer.com. To pursue a commitment to plant hundreds of ethnically diverse, self-reproducing new churches, while at the same time working for a renewal of gospel vitality in all the congregations of the city, the church founded the Redeemer Church Planting Center and recruited Dr. Osni Ferreira as its first director.

The mission of the center is to research, recruit, assess, equip, supervise, fund, and match church planters with neighborhoods in need of a vital church. The center coordinates Redeemer's effort in church planting in New York and other major urban centers of the world. It also encourages many other churches in greater New York to saturate the city with new congregations.

The immediate goal is to plant one hundred churches over the next two decades. The ultimate goal is to start and assist other churches in the birth of hundreds of additional churches in New York. Between 1993 and 1999, Redeemer planted or sponsored the planting of thirteen churches in the greater New York area, including Portuguese-, Spanish-, Chinese- and Russian-speaking congregations. Since October of 2001 alone, Redeemer has planted fourteen churches—five of its own, five with partnerships and alliances in the New York area, and four globally.

The center operates in four spheres, depending on the area and approach. In the greater New York area, it plants daughter churches while partnering with other churches and denominations to plant churches. In North America, it forms partnerships with other churches to start urban congregations in key cities. In global cities, it establishes partnerships with national churches and leaders to develop church-planting movements in major cities.

Because of its commitment to urban ministry, the center is developing training curriculums designed specifically for pastors called to multicultural planting within New York City. The Church Planting Center is funded by Redeemer Church, other churches, individuals, businesses, and foundations.

The center currently oversees sixteen church planters working in greater

New York from Wall Street to the Columbia University area and from Queens to Newark, and it assists the Metro New York Presbytery in training its church planters. It intends to plant ten new churches by the time this book is published. Redeemer has a great video on the vision and mission of the church that can be viewed right on the front page of its Web site. The video encapsulates the center's purpose: to renew the city socially, spiritually, and culturally.

Antioch Bible Church

Since its beginning in 1984, Antioch Bible Church in Redmond, Washington—led by pastors Ken (Hutch) Hutcherson and Mark Webster—has had a vision to reproduce multiethnic, cross-cultural churches for all people (see Acts 11 and 13; the church's Web site is www.abchurch.org). They want churches that reflect the surrounding community in every way instead of a church in which one type of person worships at one hour and another type worships at a different hour. They look for church planters who not only have a heart for such ministry but also have modeled it in their relationships—and are teachable so they can grow even deeper in this form of ministry.

> *"Wherever God plants a church, everybody in the area should be reflected in the gathering on Sunday. This goes beyond a color issue. We're talking about welcoming and loving the Samaritan that no one else wants."*
> —Ken (Hutch) Hutcherson
> Antioch Bible Church

In June of 1991, Greg Kappas was called to be pastor of the church-planting ministry. Since that time Antioch Bible Church has trained over two hundred church planters and has been involved in the planting of over a hundred and fifty churches, thirty-five of which are their own church plants (daughter, granddaughter, and associational church plants), as well as dozens more in various denominations. Mars Hill Church, mentioned earlier in conjunction with the Acts 29 Network, is one of these church plants. As of this writing, around seven thousand people worship in Antioch's thirty-five church plants each week.

Apparently only one of these 150-plus plants has not survived, and plans are underway to restart that church. When asked about the key to their fruitfulness, Greg Kappas said, "We carefully assess the planter and the team to ensure they are called. We then intensely train the planter and team and tenaciously coach the planter and key leaders in the first years of planting."

Three critical factors drive their ability to reach all groups. The first is an open attitude toward worship arts. Their worship leaders must have a respect for diversity in music so that all groups can relate to the worship style. Unlike certain other movements that design worship arts for a micro-culture, Antioch approaches worship as a way to include all people groups. Second, the staff must be about the business of developing intentional relationships amid many cultures. If this is achieved, the barriers that separate the groups come down. Third, the staff must be cross-cultural because the church will look like the staff.

> *"We hire people who have in their spiritual DNA a vision for a church-planting movement, not just starting a church. We are looking for spiritual reproducers who start churches to start churches that start churches. This is heavily about leadership development."*
> —Greg Kappas
>   Antioch Bible Church

The Antioch Global Network (AGN) includes the Church Planting Institute and the International Church Planters Summit, which partner with Cascade Bible College, Antioch's school that ministers with many churches. The AGN, directed by Ravon Johnson, focuses on church planting, church revitalization, and leadership development (see www.antiochglobalnetwork.org).

The Church Planting Institute (CPI) was developed because of a growing need to find and train a constituency of church planters. The purpose of the institute is "to train leaders to start multiethnic/cross-cultural churches throughout the world that become the center of community life and display to the world a true picture of the reconciling power of the Gospel of Jesus Christ." The CPI does most of the formal training. Plus, it uses both the church and the church plants as labs for the church planters.

They offer four hands-on training tracks, ranging from three months (short-term interns) to three years, depending on where the church planters are in their development. Interns spend time in ministry at Antioch Church, where they receive leadership training, visibility, and evaluation. Interns serve on the staff of the mother church and two or three church plants in order to get the real-life training of day-to-day new church development. They also receive training through Cascade Bible College and Western Seminary.

Once the location for a new plant is determined, the intern must develop a written plan of action, including a timeline. This strategic plan is referred to often and is a primary tool in coaching and accountability. Ongoing coaching is a major emphasis at Antioch. Each planter is assigned a coach when sent out to plant. Coaching consists of monthly mentoring by phone, periodic on-site visits, and regular e-mail contact.

Antioch expects four results from its training: (1) that leaders will reproduce themselves, (2) that all of their new church plants will start three to five churches within a decade so that they become reproducing churches, (3) that their planters will be faithful and fruitful, and (4) that all the church plants will have the DNA of a church for all people.

Antioch's church-planting mission is funded by outside donors, grants, a percentage of funds from church plants, and Antioch Bible Church's budget. Each church plant is expected to give a small percentage of its operating budget back to the AGN in addition to a very small fee for annual dues. Along with the AGN, each plant designates which new church plant it wants its investment to support. The AGN supports each daughter church by offering a matching gift of up to $65,000 over three years (and lesser amounts to granddaughter and associational churches).

The formation of long-term relationships is high on Antioch's agenda. It sees the mentoring/coaching to be as much about friendship and lifestyle as training. They believe this emphasis on lifestyle friendship is one of the reasons so many people gravitate to Antioch's church-planting mission.

New Hope Christian Fellowship

Wayne Cordeiro, pastor of the six-year-old New Hope Christian Fellowship, in Oahu, has been at the forefront of the church-planting movement (see www.enewhope.org). While at his previous church in Hilo, Hawaii, he started seven churches. When he moved to Oahu to begin New Hope Christian Fellowship, the passion to plant new churches still burned strong, making him one of the early apostolic leaders of our time. The goal of New Hope Fellowship is to start a hundred churches by 2010. Their hope is to plant four churches a year for the next eight years, with each existing church reproducing itself every five years.

In order to accomplish this goal, New Hope established New Hope International (see www.enhi.org/main.html), a church-growth and -planting movement affiliated with the International Church of the Foursquare Gospel. Their mission is "to fulfill the Great Commission in increasing ways through identifying and developing emerging leaders who will plant and lead effective twenty-first–century churches and assisting current ministries in increasing their effectiveness in reaching the lost."

NHI has four primary teaching arenas: Emerging Leaders International, the School of Church Planting, Pacific Rim College, and Bethel Seminary. Emerging Leaders International is a discipleship program that provides leadership training and personal mentoring in the field. It identifies, trains, and deploys young pastors for twenty-first–century ministry.

The School of Church Planting is a one- to two-year program, depending on prior experience, for leaders who plan on planting within two years. The training for full-time students combines twenty hours a week of classroom learning with laboratory work serving in the ministries of New Hope. The goal of the two years is for the planters to learn the techniques of *Doing Church as a Team*[1] and to see the heart that makes New Hope Church "tick." They are expected to develop a written plan of action before attending the SCP.

The school emphasizes character building. During the final year of their training, the planters learn how to raise their support, and the church reserves the money for them in a separate account until they leave to plant. In addition, NHI gives them a gift to begin the church when they leave.

Two more organizations make up the church-planting arsenal of New Hope International. The Pacific Rim Bible College was started to raise up leaders to plant twenty-first–century churches. The Bethel Seminary partnership was started to provide graduate-level courses for New Hope International church planters.

The planters receive coaching from NHI for a year following planting. After that, they are turned over to the church-growth side of New Hope International. NHI also provides semiannual fellowship gatherings of all the planters. Kevin Darrough is the director of the School of Church Planters, and Dan Shima is the director for church growth.

The unique aspect of NHI is its emphasis on teams. They feel that when a church planter fully understands the concept and dynamics of doing church as a team, the chances for success in the ministry—and in perseverance—are greatly enhanced. Part of the value of doing church as a team is having the people do the work of the ministry and having the pastor support the people. This form of ministry not only disciples the church but reaches out to the surrounding communities. The team concept is so ingrained that they expect each church to begin with a pastor, administrator, and worship/arts director.

NHI supports itself through grants from other organizations, gifts from other NHI churches and individuals, and a grant from New Hope Oahu. Although NHI does not guarantee any support once the planter is trained, if the church plant is Foursquare, it receives $20,000 from the denomination.

As of now, New Hope International has relationships with seventy-five churches in the Pacific Rim, the continental U.S., and Europe, and has planted fifty-five churches, most of which are Foursquare Gospel Churches. So far, all of their church plants have prevailed. Like NorthWood, New Hope planted four of the original congregations within fifteen minutes of the mother church and plans to plant more congregations on the island of Oahu.

Timeout!

For directional leaders:

- How has reading about these churches and their church-planting visions affected you?

- What does God seem to be saying to you about your ministry in the future?

For congregational leaders:

Considering how God has blessed your congregation in the past, what would be a God-sized vision for your church in the future?

- If it's not in church planting, what would it be?

Let's Talk Essentials!

As we've done in previous chapters, we'd like to distill some practical principles from the examples we've offered. We begin by asking, "What essential qualities seem to pervade the multiplication movement and its congregations?" Here are some of our observations:

Essential Quality 1: Passion for the Great Commission. Above all else, the leaders of the church-planting movements exhibit a passion for the fulfillment of the Great Commission. While the systems they develop are important, it is their commitment to the mission of transformation of individuals and communities that makes the difference. This explains some of the high failure rates among mainline denominations in both recruiting church planters and establishing effective new churches. Mainliners focus too much on the purchase of land and development and preservation of their institutions instead of participating in the fulfillment of the Great Commission. When our mainline friends return to the passion for the Great Commission and kingdom expansion, we believe they will see more fruit from their planting efforts.

In carrying out the Great Commission, these leaders focus on adult transformation. Early on in the planting process, they embed adult transformation and growth into their DNA and develop systems that encourage adults to grow spiritually. Even so, these churches have some of the finest ministries to children and youth we've seen. They just aren't the primary focus, as is often the case in other congregations.

These movements expect each new church to plant other churches or become church-planting centers. Mere survival is not the goal. Multiplication and exponential growth in the number of individual churches and church-planting centers is the goal. Each planter is trained to plant a church and develop a church-planting center. More than anything else, this passion for multiplication rather than addition is what separates these movements from most, if not all, denominational efforts in church planting. The heroes of the movement are not just leaders who go out and plant one congregation but those who mentor and train multiple church-planting teams.

Essential Quality 2: Intense leadership training. It is impossible to experience these leaders and congregations without witnessing the intensity of the selection, training, mentoring, and coaching of the church planters. These organizations invest months to years in the development and deployment of their planters. For example, New Hope International spends $2,000 a month for twenty-four months for each church planter in training. When we asked Wayne Cordeiro, pastor of New Hope Christian Fellowship, to identify the top challenge facing the church-planting movement, he replied, "Many are zealous, but we need the called ones who are willing to risk it all for the kingdom. It cannot be another 'job'; it must be a vocation where we abandon everything else. We can plant churches, but if the leadership is not the best, we will only be proliferating a low-wattage program that will not be able to light up the world."

The investment of time by these groups doesn't end when the planter plants. These organizations offer ongoing coaching, networking, and fellowship for the planters after they have planted. Their experience has shown that the first two years of a church plant are critical, and, therefore, it is important to continue to offer monitoring and mentoring by trained coaches. These movements have learned that if the first two years don't go well, more than likely neither will the ensuing years. Often, these coaches are other successful church planters in the area. Most of the planting movements link up the planter and coach. It is easy to see why the success rate of these movements far outstrips that of most denominational plants in which more money is invested in property than in training and follow-up is seldom provided.

All of the churches have internships. It's not unusual for the training to begin simply by having planters-in-training spend time in a healthy congregation to observe how healthy church leaders function. During this time the planters-in-training learn practical ministry skills through hands-on experience with seasoned veteran planters. When the time is right, the planters-in-training are given the opportunity to lead a ministry and be evaluated. Most of the centers require the church planter to identify a specific area in which to plant and draw up a prospectus complete with financials, methodology, and timelines.

Apprenticeship trumps academics.

After as much as two or three years, the planters-in-training are sent out to plant a reproducing church center. This on-the-job training is one of the key distinctives of the movement. Again, apprenticeship trumps academics. While other systems rely on educational institutions to teach a course on church planting, the multiplication movement combines the course and the real-life, hands-on training for a total process.

We are not necessarily referring to formal academic training as much as on-the-job training and modeling by the leaders in the planting centers and in the church plants. Whereas some of the planting centers are connected to a seminary, many of the church planters have little or no formal seminary training.

These church planters are trained and equipped to present the good news of God in Christ in the language, technology, and culture of the emerging world. This means that the architects of this new movement are steeped not only in Scripture but also in the culture in which they are planting the congregation. They not only have an intimate relationship with Jesus Christ, but they also have a close relationship with the secular culture.

> The architects of this new movement are steeped not only in Scripture but also in the culture in which they are planting the congregation.

All of the examples we've studied have similar aspects of training, such as assessing, coaching, modeling, mentoring, and equipping. However, not all of them emphasize these equally. The only aspect that seems to be emphasized equally is the amount of time and energy invested in the actual training of the church planters.

And because, other than prayer, entrepreneurial church planters are the key to church planting, recruitment of such church planters is a top priority. These groups look everywhere for candidates—seminaries, church plants, their own congregations and denominations, their Web sites, and simple word of mouth. These organizations spend time, energy, and money recruiting gifted and called planters within and across denominational lines. Some have in-house farm systems that raise up, train, and deploy church planters from their congregations and church plants. The staff is trained to look for potential planters everywhere they speak. Some of the churches provide CDs and printed materials that help leaders decide if church planting is their call. Most of the movements have regular gatherings or conferences where they bring together people who have an interest in church planting.

Note that most of these examples include the spouses in the training. Failure is almost assured if the spouse is not onboard and part of the team. Omitting the spouse from the training is another reason that many mainline attempts are doomed from the beginning.

These movements set high standards and expectations for their planters and have some form of partnership or covenant with them before assisting them with funds. They help to ensure the success of the plant by giving the planters guidelines and benchmarks and eliminating candidates who have a casual or romantic interest in church planting. In addition, most of these centers require the church planter to have an action plan and clearly identified mission, vision, and values before beginning the planting journey. Requiring such an intensive commitment of time and energy weeds out many church-planting candidates and ensures more successful plants.

Essential Quality 3: Cross-pollination among the groups. We were impressed with the emphasis on cross-pollination among all of these groups. The groups blend their efforts together in order to avoid the "Paul and Apollos syndrome" found in 1 Corinthian 3. Most of the examples we've cited are so intertwined with one another that at times it's difficult to tell the groups apart. Many of the churches send their interns to visit other church-planting centers to ensure that they are not just developing clones, experience another form of training, and instill in them the importance of developing community and relationships among other church planters.

Because they understand that kingdom work is far too big for any one congregation or denomination to undertake alone, these movements form partnerships. Many of the leaders and groups network and partner with one another. The largest percentages of the partnerships occur in the sharing and training of church planters and effective methodologies.

It is impossible to over-stress the amount of collaboration we found among all of these groups. Even though the theology and methodology of these groups differ widely, we witnessed a deep respect for each group in everyone we interviewed.

Some of the groups required strict obedience to their doctrines; others did not. Some allowed only male leaders; others invited females. Some are evangelical; some are fundamentalist. Even so, each group spoke highly of the others. Mark Driscoll's comments are typical: "This is what we believe, and if you want to plant with us, this is what you have to believe. We have distinctives that are controversial, and we are unashamed of them. We acknowledge that God is also working through different people and groups who may vary from us, and we sincerely celebrate God using them. However, we also know who he has called us to be." The spirit we experienced can only happen in a kingdom environment. We hope the day will come when our mainline friends will be as open to other groups.

Essential Quality 4: Preferring the local over the denominational. Each of these congregations believes it is more biblical for the local church to plant churches than for denominations to do it. While they acknowledge the important role overseeing entities can play in church planting, they feel that many congregations have abdicated their own responsibility by not planting churches. When local churches plant churches, the whole congregation becomes involved by praying for the plants, giving to make them happen, and even in leaving the planting church to be part of the new plant. This personal involvement of the congregation can be so contagious that it adds fuel to the growth of the planting church. Denominations, wanting to effectively plant churches and cut down their high number of failures, would do well to link up with church-planting churches in their denominations and put their funds into those churches' efforts instead of trying to do it themselves.

However, our fear is that most denominations will choose to dabble in adding church plants partly because they do not have enough "kingdom attitude" to move outside their group. Or they are afraid to put too much effort into starting new congregations because they're not sure the congregations will remain loyal. Plus, they don't want to give away control. Most of the mainline denominations simply do not have enough entrepreneurial pastors to be part of a multiplication movement. The best they can hope for is to create enough new congregations to remain in existence. However, they are finding even that is next to impossible.

Our experience has taught us that too many denominational church plants fail for at least five reasons: Too few of the church planters have a kingdom view of their ministry; too few have a clear and specific call to planting a church; too few have spent much time in a thriving church, much less worked in a church plant; too few have intensive training; and too few have coaches who have planted a church.

And here is one other aspect of the preference for the local church: Most of the planting movements require their church planters to raise the funds for their plants. The thinking is that if the planters can't raise *financial* support, they probably can't raise *people* support. The average startup requires around $100,000. This is a huge difference from most denominational approaches. Very early on, many denominational systems grant new congregations significant funds for a site and pastoral support. This creates unhealthy dependencies not faced in the planting-movement approach.

Essential Quality 5: A "sooner than later" mentality. We've observed that the sooner a congregation plants a new church, the easier it is for the new church to become a planting center. Congregations that plant their first church within three to five years of their birth find that it is much easier to plant both the first church and subsequent churches. We've noticed that established churches have all kinds of hurdles to overcome before they can plant their first three or four churches. Longtime members think of multiplication as building an empire in one location by adding on to the existing campus. It takes time to change this mind-set. When churches plant at a young age, planting becomes part of the DNA much more easily and quickly.

Yet this approach requires flexibility and teachability. Much is trial and error at the beginning of these movements. Each of the leaders we interviewed was more than willing to make changes as needs arose. According to Max Wikins, teaching pastor and director of edification at New Hope, "We do church planting on the fly. There are no real rules, and everything is subject to change, moment by moment. Even in the few cases where we have some minimal unwritten guidelines, we throw them aside in an instant if a good opportunity requires it."

Teachability is an asset for church planters who are quickly jumping into the multiplication movement. While none of the movements downplayed formal education, most would rather recruit someone with little education and a big passion than someone with impressive degrees who isn't passionate about—and clearly called to—church planting. They would also rather imprint their own methodologies on a blank slate than to have to deprogram someone who has been filled with unusable information and experience.

Essential Quality 6: A willingness to sacrifice—at all levels. Planting congregations sacrifice time, energy, and money in the pursuit of reproducing churches. The people being trained seldom directly benefit the planting congregation. Often, after months of investment in a candidate, the person doesn't work out or proves to be called to some other form of ministry. (In such cases, often the planting congregation will help the person find a place in ministry.) Even the new church plants are asked to give and sacrifice. Early in their development, the new church plants give away staff and money to help plant other churches.

Even the vision of a huge mega-church gets sacrificed to more kingdom-oriented concerns. Size just doesn't matter to these folks. They focus more on intimate community and servant development. Instead of becoming land developers, they focus on developing people.

All too often in church-planting circles of the past, congregations first focused on a building or location, not a community of people. So from the start the plant was either in debt, chronically short of money, or unable to quickly relocate if necessary.

But the multiplication movement moves beyond those boxes, and it's here to stay. We feel this trend will not only continue but will also escalate with time.

Timeout!

For directional and congregational leaders:

• If you are planting already, which of the essential qualities needs to be strengthened among you? Where are your "weakest links" beginning to appear? What can you do about them?

• If you aren't planting yet but are considering it, which one of the essential qualities excites you the most? Which causes you to flinch the hardest? Why?

What Are the Ongoing Challenges?

Historically, movements tend to wane with the passing of their founders. Church-planting movements face the same future unless they intentionally and continually focus on planting churches that become church-planting centers. They must not allow the organization itself to become the focus of attention.

It will be interesting to see whether, over the years, more emphasis is placed on the organization than the actual planting. If history is any predictor, refusing to allow the organizational tail to wag the church-planting dog will be the greatest challenge facing these movements. We hope that the visionary leadership will call on a leader in one of the daughter or granddaughter churches to take up the cause and that new centers will rise up from the daughter and granddaughter family trees. The DNA to start new movements runs deep within these movements.

The most immediate challenge is the number of church planters these movements are able to recruit and develop. Not everyone wants to (or is able to) plant churches. The number of new churches these movements can plant is limited only by the amount of money they can raise and the number of qualified and called church planters they can find. It's evident from our interviews that the leaders of these movements are well aware of this challenge. Yet one bright spot is that the more new church plants are begun, the more new church planters will emerge because, as much as anything, the culture in which new converts grow up sets the stage for God's calling of more planters. A leadership-oriented culture tends to beget more leaders.

However, a small-church mentality can be a real obstacle here. To many church leaders, the church exists primarily as a fixed, single, isolated group of people. Their actions show little if any understanding of the biblical picture of a church or the kingdom mentality. They put their energies into the survival or effectiveness of their local congregations, so they can't conceive of using some of their hard-won funds or giving away some of their best members to plant another church. That would weaken their church, right? Somehow, over the long haul, all of us have allowed such thinking to run rampant. We must begin seeing the world as our parish and the church next door as a potential partner in furthering the kingdom. We are not in competition with other Christians!

We are not in competition with other Christians!

But will denominational judicatories get on board? It seems that their attitude often has two facets: One is *negative* and the other is *fearful.* Some judicatories simply don't think it is the role of churches to plant churches. They feel planting should be left up to the denomination. Others don't even see the value in planting congregations because they lack passion for the fulfillment of the Great Commission. Some are against congregational or parachurch planting because they fear losing control of their constituencies.

We have interviewed hundreds of denominational officials, both evangelical and mainline, and the vast majority of these leaders appear to be so concerned about the survival of their own groups that they are oblivious to the absolute imperative of expanding the kingdom. As long as they focus on denominational survival, their future is bleak. God simply does not honor that kind of an attitude.

Finally, the church-planting movement will face three other challenges, each of which could slow down multiplication. As the world continues to change, the quality and content of the training will have to continually change and improve. As the number of new church plants increases, the need for more experienced and willing coaches will also increase. As the stability of the modern world continues to unravel, the need for support structures for church planters will increase. These issues must be addressed for the movement to continue. (We hope that in a future book, we can address a variety of church-planting styles and methodologies with their respective strengths and weaknesses.)

Even with these challenges, we believe the future is bright for the multiplication movement because it is a "God thing" in every respect. God honors those who stretch and push in order to expand the kingdom. May the church-planting movements continue to expand until everyone has heard the good news!

Timeout!

For directional and congregational leaders:

Assuming you are either into the planting movement or are considering it...

• Which of the challenges might be the hardest to address? Why? What have you learned from this chapter that will help you address it?

Endnote

1. For further reading about teams, see Wayne Cordeiro's *Doing Church as a Team* (Ventura, CA: Regal Books, 2001).

Epilogue

Beyond Minding the Store

We've examined five of the leadership and ministry issues we believe are key to setting the course for the future church. We pray that they have captured your spirit. We'd like to think that your imagination has been ignited. And we definitely hope you're ready to move beyond whatever box hinders your participation in these movements of the kingdom.

By now you should be aware that two words are essential to understanding these issues—*movement* and *multiplication*. Everything beyond-the-box leaders do flows from these two concepts. They focus on contributing to a larger movement rather than growing a single institution. All of their efforts go into exponentially self-multiplying rather than merely growing by addition. This focus, more than anything else, separates the effective and fruitful leaders from those who are simply "minding the store."

It should also be obvious by now that these leaders are wired differently than most leaders of the recent past. Since they have a beyond-the-box mind-set, we need to ask ourselves, "What are the common threads of this mind-set?"

What Are These Leaders Like?

On the one hand, we didn't find many transferable commonalties. Each church and leader we studied develops unique ways to do ministry. And that's the first lesson we need to heed. The further we go into the future, the less likely it is that successful approaches will transfer from one church or location to another. That's what's so troubling to most of the declining denominations and so many church leaders. They still insist that one size fits all. However, none of what we found can be thought of as an approach or program that other churches can merely copy wholesale. The day of generic, cookie-cutter programs is ending. This conclusion may disappoint some of you because you are still within the box. We suggest that it's time to climb out of the box.

On the other hand, if you look beyond the box, you can indeed see some distinguishing, transferable passions and characteristics within this new mind-set. In discussing these traits, we'll refer primarily to the qualities of the leaders themselves. A form of apostolic leader is emerging that we have not seen in a long time. These leaders are modern-day versions of Paul, and they are essential to beyond-the-box approaches. Their primary responsibility is to the movement they have spawned more than to the church out of which the movement began. They are shifting from being the pastors of churches to being the apostles of regions. They focus on building leadership teams wherever they go. We believe these apostles are tomorrow's leaders, and we expect to see their numbers grow.

1. Each leader has a specific call from God.

We emphasize *specific* rather than *generic*. Unlike many Christian leaders who feel called to "ministry" and are comfortable in a variety of institutional settings, these leaders are crystal clear about exactly what God wants them to do—and how they can participate in the fulfillment of the Great Commission. They sense that they can do nothing else but what they are doing in serving the kingdom movement.

Ken (Hutch) Hutcherson, pastor of Antioch Bible Church, sums up this passion as well as anyone we interviewed. At the first meeting of the people he invited to join him in planting Antioch, he said, "If this doesn't go, I'm going to close the doors. Either we're going to be obedient to God, or we are going to close the doors."

Ken was referring to his call from God to plant a church for all people. What he meant was that if *this* church didn't reflect the surrounding community in every way, he would actually close the church down. Ken had a very specific calling. He was to plant a church in which all people are respected, loved, and welcomed with open arms, regardless of race, situation in life, and social status.

> *"Acts 29 has only been around a few years and has learned a lot. I do believe the thousand churches God has laid on my heart will happen by his grace in my lifetime, and I can now see it unfolding before me."*
> —Mark Driscoll

Timeout!

For directional leaders:

• What is God's specific call on your life? How do you articulate this call in your daily life? How is it directing your leadership in practical ways?

• Is your call setting the agenda, or is the church you're serving setting the agenda? How can you tell?

• Where do you see a match between your call and the church? Where do you see tensions between the two?

For congregational leaders:

• How would you go about discerning God's *specific* call on your church and its ministry? Where is the evidence pointing?

• What processes could you use to begin seeking insight into your specific calling? How might this book help you?

2. Each leader moves forward with a kingdom mentality.

How can we describe this mentality? A story from Bob Roberts should help: "We were going faster in reverse than we had ever gone in drive. It was embarrassing, humiliating. And it was the best thing that ever happened to us."

That's how Bob describes a defining moment for the church he founded—NorthWood Church in Keller, Texas. The year was 1992. NorthWood was seven years old and would have been considered very successful by most standards. The church had grown from fewer than fifty people to nearly five hundred, and it was moving into a prime shopping-center location. NorthWood's future was bright and promising, but Pastor Roberts knew a problem existed, both in himself and his people.

When his congregation made an earlier decision to relocate to a shopping center, about a hundred and fifty people decided *not* to move with it. "Everybody voted in the meetings to make the move. But they voted differently with their feet," Roberts says. With that 30 percent downturn in attendance almost overnight, Bob went into a tailspin that God would use to change the trajectory of his life and ministry.

Roberts describes the turning point this way: "I was walking around in my back yard, and I was griping at God. I kept saying things like 'God, if we just had fifty more people there, I would be happy. If we had just one hundred more people there, I would be happy.'"

When will Jesus be enough for you?

Then this little question came into his mind: "Bob, when will Jesus be enough for you?"

He realized for the first time that Jesus hadn't been enough. He wept when this realization hit him.

Bob Roberts' ministry and church would never be the same after that day of spiritual and mental transformation. He began to realize that if Jesus really was enough, then Jesus' kingdom had to reign supreme over all Bob's goals, hopes, and dreams for NorthWood. Bob became obsessed with the kingdom. This was the beginning of NorthWood's journey into the church-planting movement. God had given a specific kingdom mission to Bob that he couldn't refuse.

Most pastors within the box don't see any difference in their call and what we've just described. That's sad. The best advice here is to climb out of your box long enough to spend time with beyond-the-box leaders, and the difference will become clear. You've spent too much of your time around the normal, run of the mill, institutional pastor and congregation.

Timeout!

For directional and congregational leaders:

• When was the last time you visited a church you would describe as either out of the box or beyond the box? What were your impressions?

• **They have a kingdom view of the community.** These leaders aren't content with having their congregations reach their communities. They want their churches to be *in* their communities, relating to them, loving them, and transforming them. In biblical fashion, they are concerned with more than just personal salvation. They are concerned also with changing the environment within the community. They pray for their communities. They walk the streets of their communities. They work with community leaders from all walks of life. They are *in* the world without being *of* the world. And their presence is making a difference.

Timeout!

For directional leaders:

• What is the level of your kingdom mentality? What evidence supports your response?

For congregational leaders:

• What is the level of your church's kingdom mentality? In what ways can you take an accurate, in-depth assessment in the weeks ahead?

• **They release the people.** We're talking about a "release mentality." Leadership development is at the heart of ministry for these leaders. They exist to equip, empower, and set all of God's people into ministry within and beyond the congregation. Whether it is giving people away to plant a new church or giving up centralized power in favor of the power of the many, these leaders shun micromanagement and controlling mechanisms.

Similarly, they never think only of what they can accomplish or what their churches can accomplish. Neither are they concerned with addition because they know it will take much more to fulfill the Great Commission. Instead, they think of what would be possible if the whole body of Christ were equipped, mobilized, and released for spiritual warfare.

They truly have taken the message to heart that "it is more blessed to give away than to receive." In trying to give as much as they can of themselves, their churches, their churches' resources, and their personal influence, they are blessed in ways they could never have imagined. Does this mean numerical and financial loss for their churches? Sometimes it does. But by releasing what God has directed them to release, they are blessed later to better serve their call and vision in those communities.

• **Their hearts are called to serve.** These pastors universally exhibit servants' hearts. A prime example comes from New Hope in Oahu. Everyone has to begin ministry at New Hope by demonstrating *a willingness to serve*. As a result, almost everyone who has a desire to do paid ministry must "enter through the servant's entrance." All those who appear to have a call to ministry are first offered the chance to volunteer in the church or to raise their own support and intern with New Hope.

Often new people begin by being a Levite (those who set up for worship each weekend, in the middle of the night). Someone will suggest to a new person that "the Levites could really use some help" and then drop it, step back, and see if they have the heart to serve. Very few people are pursued as church planters until they have first demonstrated a heart to serve—*and* demonstrated fruit from that service.

The surest way *not* to plant a New Hope church is to announce that you are interested in church planting. Those people who get busy, produce in ministry, and seem to have good hearts are then often approached with the idea of church planting. And many respond favorably. Even when Kevin Darrough, Director of the School of Church Planting, actively recruits church planters, the potential planters are approached based on their *demonstrated* skills and calling.

• **They have an unlimited vision of the ministry.** Since they see what they are doing as a "God thing," these leaders are convinced that all things are possible. Personal spiritual disciplines come easier with that perspective on the world. Prayer, daily obedience, and Scripture reading become the fabric of the person, with an unlimited kingdom vision flowing from the soul. A prime example of this is the Shadowing Practicum of Wayne Cordeiro. Several times a year, a handful of pastors spend a week following Wayne around, beginning in the early hours of the morning for prayer, devotional time, and physical exercise.

Because of their reliance on God, these leaders are largely unencumbered by baggage from the past. That is what makes them unique and so refreshing. Are they conservative? The majority are. Are they fundamentalists? Some are. A few are more liberal. But all of them are open to working with anyone who is into multiplication in order to fulfill the Great Commission. This takes them far, far away from much of the present-day denominational idolatry.

The kind of vision and passion we've seen in these leaders and churches can't be taught. Nor is it the result of some form of psychological motivation. It's a passion that comes from one's relationship with God. It's a passion to fulfill the Great Commission. It's a passion to bring the world into a relationship with Jesus Christ. Such passion is what separates these churches from the vast majority of others.

Timeout!

For directional and congregational leaders:

- How would you describe the "release factor" in your church?

- Is your organization designed mostly to control what people do or mostly to release them into ministry? What is the evidence for your answer?

3. Each leader partners on the basis of mission alone.

At a time when many pastors fellowship only with those within their denominations, these leaders are seeing beyond the box of denomination—or even theology—to the primacy of the mission to which they are called. When pastors become servants to a broader vision of God's work in a community, everything changes. They go from leading only their churches to serving God's vision in partnership with other pastors and churches.

The formation of Acts 29 is an excellent example of such partnering. When they met, both Mark Driscoll and David Nicholas had successful ministries. At the age of twenty-seven, Mark had planted Mars Hill, Seattle, in the fall of 1997, and within two years began planting other churches. Mark felt a call to commit his life to preaching the gospel and planting one thousand churches.

Through a friend, Mark was introduced to Dr. David Nicholas at Spanish River Church in Florida. Mark was twenty-nine; David was sixty-nine. Mark had been in ministry full-time for two years; David had been in ministry for over thirty years. Mark wasn't affiliated with a denomination; David was Presbyterian. Mark wasn't seminary trained; David had a doctorate in theology. Mark was reaching postmoderns; David was reaching moderns. The two had little in common except their shared love for the gospel and a heart for church planting.

Twenty years before this, David and his church had developed the Spanish River Network, which had funded the planting of eighty-four Presbyterian churches in the United States and around the world. Mark joined this network and began bringing in non-seminary–trained pastors who weren't necessarily Presbyterian and were generally younger than the Presbyterian pastors.

Seeing the inevitable tensions that would arise from trying to fold emerging planters in with traditional planters, David risked everything, including his reputation, and cancelled the successful Spanish River Network. Together, Mark and David began a new network called Acts 29. David and Mark are an unlikely pair of disciples, drawn together by mission. Such a partnership doesn't mean that everything always unfolds with rosy sweetness. Disagreements and conflicts arise, but a passion for the mission seems always to prevail.

4. Each leader demonstrates "strategic mapping."

Because they are sailing uncharted waters, none of these leaders has or follows a strategic plan. Instead, they have a clear destination in mind and make up their strategic map as they go. Think of strategic mapping not as a highway map that says "this way" or "turn here" but as a topographical map in which explorers and surveyors fill in the hazards, the terrain, the canyons, the streams—the contour lines of the culture. They make up a lot of it as they go.

For these leaders, methodology is relatively unimportant compared to the one driving criterion: Does it transform people and community? The methods they use all depend on what they determine, at any moment in time, will produce the largest harvest.

New Hope began with a vision to plant new congregations in difficult places along the Pacific Rim. Having outgrown their space in Honolulu, they opened two new satellite churches in January of 2003 for a total of four locations. These new satellites have been so successful that they're considering opening additional satellites in the near future. They reason that a church plant will reach two to three hundred people on average, whereas multiple sites in the area can reach two or three times as many people and allow continued expansion without spending millions of dollars to build a facility large enough to house a single congregation.

In the same way, when Pastor Cordeiro retires or moves into another area of ministry, the church will have several options for replacing him. How it is done is not nearly as important to these leaders as achieving the mission.

5. These leaders concentrate on people, not programs.

Rather than developing programs to involve people, these leaders focus on intensive, on-the-job modeling for everyone in their congregations. Leaders at every level are equipped and encouraged to carry out the Great Commission, not just to be theologians. Their primary learning lab is found in the challenges that confront them and the ways they handle those challenges. These leaders may be well educated, but more than anything, they are capable of adaptive, on-the-journey learning. All of the leaders we interviewed consider mentoring, modeling, and coaching to be vital parts of their roles.

Most of the churches we studied have a two-pronged approach to equipping. On the one hand, they teach a curriculum, and on the other hand, they do intense modeling through relationships and on-the-job experience. It is the combination of the two that makes the difference. Most in-the-box churches think that all they have to do is purchase a program and run a study in order to produce disciples. Not so. People have to be personally touched by discipleship in action before they can be transformed.

These congregations have radically decentralized everything in order to facilitate the exponential exploration of new and better ways to expand the kingdom. They know that the more decentralized they are, the easier it is to expand ministry as rapidly as opportunities present themselves. They would rather risk some complexity and confusion along the way than try to control their contribution to the growth of the kingdom. Radically decentralizing facilitates growth of the individual, the congregation, and the kingdom.

What's Keeping You in the Box?

Clearly, no matter what else these leaders are doing, they are developing teams and a culture of equipping in which everyone is considered a leadership candidate.[1] Many of the churches are crossing over between multiple-site and planting churches. All of the churches have some tentacles into the community at large with a view to changing it.

In other words, a new DNA is emerging among the beyond-the-box churches that is much more in tune with first-century Christianity than we have seen for sixteen or more centuries. Yet many churches will not, or cannot, get beyond the box. Why? Consider two of the greatest obstacles.

The first major obstacle is that most in-the-box pastors function more as caregivers than as leaders. Many pastors actually entered ministry in order to take care of others with no thought of discipling them. As one pastor told us, "If I did what you're recommending, there wouldn't be any reason for me to be a minister. I entered *the* ministry *because I thought people needed me.*"

If you ask these chaplain-type pastors how they spend most of their time, they won't show you hours of equipping or modeling the faith to interns. Nor will they talk about multiplication. Rather, you see them visiting hospitals, seeing shut-ins, refereeing institutional conflicts, teaching non-reproducing Bible studies, preaching to the churched, and hoping their individual churches survive.

The vast majority of pastors are chaplains, not leaders. They serve a particular flock rather than participating in a great community. They have an institutional rather than a kingdom mind-set. They take Jesus' words about feeding his sheep out of context, because shepherds don't actually *feed* sheep. Instead, they make sure the sheep are in a safe environment in which they can eat, grow, and reproduce more sheep.

Shepherds don't beget sheep. Sheep beget sheep.

In order to move beyond the box, pastors must give up the chaplain approach to ministry. Rather than viewing themselves as caregivers, they must think of themselves as missionaries, apostles, change agents, and kingdom builders.

The second major obstacle is fear. The five aspects of a beyond-the-box mentality that we've explored are mostly unknown to traditional church leaders, and just the mention of them strikes fear into many. But "there is no fear in love" (1 John 4:18a). To become beyond-the-box leaders and overcome their fears, pastors must fall more deeply in love with Jesus Christ.[2]

Pastors, perhaps it's time to fall more in love with what God is doing in the world than to continue being enamored with the comfort and security of your present situation. At every key point in history, God has raised up courageous men and women to continue to advance the kingdom. It's true in our time. God is calling you to a specific form of kingdom mission. Isn't it time to take stock and respond?

If the way we see twenty-first–century Christianity shaping up is anywhere close to reality, then we may be witnessing the rebirth of scriptural Christianity and the beginning of the fulfillment of the Great Commission. Are you ready to do your part?

Endnotes

1. For more on every person being considered a potential leader, see Bill Easum's *Leadership on the OtherSide: No Rules, Just Clues* (Nashville: Abingdon Press, 2000).
2. In their book *Growing Spiritual Redwoods*, Bill Easum and Thomas Bandy ask this question: "What is it about your relationship with Jesus Christ that the world cannot live without knowing?"

Appendix
Resources You Can Use

Chapter 1

On general shifts in thinking about teams

Barna, George, *The Power of Team Leadership: Achieving Success Through Shared Responsibility* (Colorado Springs, CO: Waterbrook Press, 2001). George has the best book in the list for an all-encompassing view on the subject, which describes the strengths and challenges as well.

George, Carl F. with Warren Bird, *The Coming Church Revolution: Empowering Leaders for the Future* (Grand Rapids, MI: Fleming H. Revell Co., 1994). Though written primarily for those in the meta-model, you'll find good thoughts here on sharing the ministry and setting up teams.

Sweet, Leonard, *AquaChurch: Essential Leadership Arts for Piloting Your Church in Today's Fluid Culture* (Loveland, CO: Group Publishing, Inc., 1999). Chapter 9, " Valuing the Crew: Collaboration and Teamwork," is especially relevant to this topic.

Wagner, C. Peter, *The New Apostolic Churches* (Ventura, CA: Regal Books, 2000).

Osborne, Larry W., *The Unity Factor: Developing a Healthy Church Leadership Team* (Vista, CA: Owl's Nest, 2001). Larry is featured in this chapter. These articles originally appeared in Leadership Journal. You'll find some of the best information on church-board development in his section two.

Ott, E. Stanley, *Twelve Dynamic Shifts for Transforming Your Church* (Grand Rapids, MI: Wm. B. Eerdmans Publishing Co., 2002). Stan's book is a good primer for mainline leaders covering shifts occurring in the church. Pay special attention to the chapter titled "Shifts in the Practice of Leadership."

On developing teams

Bandy, Thomas G., *Coaching Change: Breaking Down Resistance, Building Up Hope* (Nashville, TN: Abingdon Press, 2000). Tom is Bill Easum's ministry partner, and this book is a good primer on coaching people for change rather than demanding and driving.

Cordeiro, Wayne, *Doing Church as a Team* (Ventura, CA: Regal Books, 2001). Wayne is featured throughout this book. He tells great stories while offering a plan for developing teams and equipping leaders. He also explains his "fractal concept" in detail.

On staff leadership teams

Cladis, George, *Leading the Team-Based Church: How Pastors and Church Staffs Can Grow Together into a Powerful Fellowship of Leaders* (San Francisco, CA: Jossey-Bass, 1999). Cladis focuses on the covenants and commitments a staff must develop with each other.

McIntosh, Gary L., *Staff Your Church for Growth: Building Team Ministry in the 21st Century* (Grand Rapids, MI: Baker Book House, 2000).

Stanley, Andy and Ed Young, *Can We Do That? 24 Innovative Practices That Will Change the Way You Do Church* (West Monroe, LA: Howard Publishing, 2002). See Chapter 17 for a good description on how staff is hired at Fellowship Church.

On the character needed to be a team leader

McNeal, Reggie, *A Work of Heart: Understanding How God Shapes Spiritual Leaders* (San Francisco, CA: Jossey-Bass, 2000). This book includes an examination of calling as it relates to a spiritual leader.

Thrall, Bill, Bruce McNicol, and Ken McElrath, *The Ascent of a Leader: How Ordinary Relationships Develop Extraordinary Character and Influence* (San Francisco, CA: Jossey-Bass, 1999).

On the role of a team in changing a church

Herrington, Jim, Mike Bonem, and James H. Furr, *Leading Congregational Change: A Practical Guide for the Transformational Journey* (San Francisco, CA: Jossey-Bass, 2000). Deals with transitioning to a team-based ministry.

Easum, Bill, *Team Based Ministry.* This is a practical workbook you can order through Easum, Bandy & Associates. Go to www.easumbandy.com.

Chapter 2

On the equipping culture, from Leadership Training Network

Mallory, Sue, *The Equipping Church: Serving Together to Transform Lives* (Grand Rapids, MI: Zondervan. 2001). This landmark book offers the philosophy and stories behind the equipping movement, based primarily on Sue's experience at Brentwood Presbyterian Church.

Mallory, Sue, Brad Smith, Sarah Jane Rehnborg, and Neil Wilson, *The Equipping Church Guidebook* (Grand Rapids, MI: Zondervan, 2001). Contains the starter kit of practical tools. Sue Mallory heads up the Leadership Training Network, which produces some of the best books and materials on this subject. The LTN approach designates a point person who helps facilitate equipping in a church.

LTN also publishes a series of training modules complete with handouts and CD-rom presentations and offers church-assessment tools. They hold regular training institutes for church-based teams that want to adapt the equipping model to their congregations. See www.ltn.org.

On team-based ministry throughout the church

Cordeiro, Wayne, *Doing Church as a Team* (Ventura, CA: Regal Books, 2001). Wayne's ministry is featured throughout this book. Also, check out the training practicum that New Hope does for pastors. You can find out more at www.enewhope.org.

On the equipping culture, in general

Ogden, Greg, *The New Reformation: Returning the Ministry to the People of God* (Grand Rapids, MI: Zondervan, 1991).

Easum, Bill, *Leadership on the OtherSide: No Rules, Just Clues* (Nashville, TN: Abingdon Press, 2000).

Slaughter, Michael with Warren Bird, *UnLearning Church: Just When You Thought You Had Leadership All Figured Out* (Loveland, CO: Group Publishing, Inc., 2001). See especially Chapter 15, "Spiritual Visionaries," which points toward the kind of leader needed in an equipping culture.

Chapter 3

Dennison, Jack, *City Reaching: On the Road to Community Transformation* (Colorado Springs, CO: Gabriel Resources, 1999). This book probably does the best job, overall, in laying out the church-in-a-city philosophy.

Haggard, Ted and Jack Hayford, *Loving Your City into the Kingdom: City-Reaching Strategies for a 21st-Century Revival* (Ventura, CA: Regal Books, 1998). See especially the story of Colorado Springs.

Lewis, Robert, *The Church of Irresistible Influence* (Grand Rapids, MI: Zondervan, 2002). Lewis tells the story of his church's pilgrimage toward addressing the whole community.

Otis, George, Jr., *Informed Intercession* (Ventura, CA: Regal Books, 1999).

Sjogren, Steve, Stephen L. Ayers, and Bob Logan, *Seeing Beyond Church Walls: Action Plans for Touching Your Community* (Loveland, CO: Group Publishing, Inc., 2001). See especially Chapter 4, "Outward-Focused Partnerships" by Tom Pelton, which gives several practical examples of kingdom-based ministries.

Guder, Darrell L., *The Continuing Conversion of the Church* (Grand Rapids, MI: Wm. B. Eerdmans Publishing Co., 2000).

Guder, Darrell L. and Lois Barrett, *Missional Church: A Vision for the Sending of the Church in North America* (Grand Rapids, MI: Wm. B. Eerdmans Publishing Co., 1998).

Some recommended Web sites

www.citireach.org.—CitiReach International

www.sentinelgroup.org—The Sentinel Group

www.nppn.org/Articles/Article%20Focus.htm.—The National Pastors Prayer Network. The site offers compilations of dozens of papers on this and related topics.

www.missionhouston.org—Mission Houston

Chapter 4

Because it is still so new, not much has been written on the multisite phenomenon. But here are some bits and pieces of helpful information that are currently available.

Galloway, Dale E., *Leading in Times of Change* (Kansas City, MO: Beacon Hill Press, 2003). See Chapter 7 on the story of First United Methodist Church of Houston, Texas, written by William Hinson.

Schaller, Lyle E., *Innovations in Ministry: Models for the 21st Century* (Nashville, TN: Abingdon Press, 1994). See the sections on off-campus ministries and the multisite option for some insight into the varieties of multisite approaches.

Pope, Randy, *The Prevailing Church: An Alternative Approach to Ministry* (Chicago, IL: Moody Press, 2002). This is the story of Perimeter Church, written by its founding pastor. He discusses the church's pilgrimage with the multisite idea.

Bowman, Ray and Eddy Hall, *When Not to Build: An Architect's Unconventional Wisdom for the Growing Church* (Grand Rapids, MI: Baker Book House, 2000).

Some recommended Web sites

Dave Travis wrote a brief white paper for Leadership Network. Find it on the Web site at www.leadnet.org under "Resources."

North Coast Church has an annual conference on the idea. See www.northcoastchurch.com to find information. They also have a Web presentation called "Starting a Video Café" at www.videocafes.org.

For more information on renting space, see www.easumbandy.com/resources/faqs and look under "renting."

Chapter 5

Books on church planting abound, but they generally describe the planting of one church at a time. These resources go beyond that box!

Moore, Ralph, *Starting a New Church* (Ventura, CA: Regal Books, 2002). This is a must-read book about methodologies similar to those mentioned in the various case studies in this chapter. The author emphasizes what this church and planter have learned after planting multiple churches.

Schaller, Lyle E., *44 Questions for Church Planters* (Nashville, TN: Abingdon Press, 1991).

Some recommended Web sites

www.dcpi.org.—The mission of Dynamic Church Planting International is "to equip leaders, churches, and associations to impact the planting of one million dynamic churches to reach the world for Christ."

www.NewChurchSpecialties.org—New Church Specialties' mission "assists the starting and strengthening of NewStart, ReStart, & ReFocusing churches worldwide."

www.cmtcmultiply.org—The Church Multiplication Training Center's mission is all about "multiplying reproducing churches by equipping and empowering church planters, spouses, and their coaches."

www.crmnet.org—Church Resource Ministries (CRM) focuses mostly on boot camps for postmodern, bivocational plants.

Kappas, Greg, and Gary Rohremayer have produced a good CD titled *Twenty-Five Questions for Planting a Healthy Church* that contains 220 MB of helpful information. You can find it at www.easumbandy.com under "Workbooks" or from Gary Rohrmayer, 319 Lake Shore Dr., Lindenhurst, IL 60046, mrohmayer@aol.com.

Conferences

Several of the churches featured in this chapter have church-planting conferences:

www.churchplanter.com—Northwest Church Planting has frequent training.

www.NorthWoodchurch.org/mission/cplant.htm—NorthWood Church in Keller, Texas, regularly holds conferences in addition to its internships.